WALTER A. HAZEN

Good Year Books

Parsippany, New Jersey

Photo Credits

Unless otherwise acknowledged, all photographs are the property of Scott, Foresman and Company. Page abbreviations are as follows: (T)top, (C)center, (B)bottom, (L)left, (R)right.
Front cover(r) Hand-colored for Scott Foresman•Addison Wesley Longman by Cheryl Kucharzak
6 Library of Congress
7(t) Corbis/Bettmann
7(b) International Harvester Company
8 Multicultural Music and Art Foundation, Northridge, CA
14 I. N. Phelps Stokes Collection/New York Public Library, Aster, Lenox and Tilden Foundation
15 Library of Congress
17, 18 Courtesy, Ford Motor Company
24 Deutsches Museum
25 Hagley Museum and Library
26 Brown Brothers
33 National Library of Medicine
34 Acme/Corbis/Bettmann
35 Corbis/Bettmann Archive
36 National Foundation for Infantile Paralysis
43 Culver Pictures Inc.
44 U. S. Army photo
49, 50 Corbis/Bettmann
52 Moore School of Engineering
57(t) Smithsonian Institution
57(b), 58 Brown Brothers
59 Henry Ford Museum and Greenfield Village
60 Culver Pictures Inc.
61 UPI/Corbis/Bettmann
66 Hand-colored for Scott Foresman•Addison Wesley Longman by Cheryl Kucharzak
67 Brown Brothers
68 Corbis/Bettmann
69(t) Culver Pictures Inc.
69(b), 77 H. Armstrong Roberts, Inc.
83 Goddard Space Flight Center/NASA
84 Sovfoto
85, 86 NASA

To Martha, Jordan, and Allison

Good Year Books
are available for most basic curriculum subjects plus many enrichment areas. For more Good Year Books, contact your local bookseller or educational dealer. For a complete catalog with information about other Good Year Books, please write:

Good Year Books
An imprint of Pearson Learning
299 Jefferson Road
Parsippany, New Jersey 07054-0480
1-800-321-3106
www.pearsonlearning.com

Design: Christine Ronan Design

Unless otherwise acknowledged,
all illustrations are by Joe Rogers.

Printed in the United States of America.

ISBN 0-673-36323-6

4 5 6 7 8 - BI - 04 03 02 01 00

Table of Contents

Table of Contents *continued*

Introduction

In the early 1900s, some people suggested that the U.S. Patent Office in Washington, D.C., be closed. Their reasoning? Everything that could be invented had been, and the need for a patent office no longer existed.

Sounds absurd, doesn't it? Obviously, the persons making such a recommendation were neither inventors nor scientists. The true inventor knows that progress and new ideas will continue as long as people populate the earth.

In *Everyday Life: Inventions,* you will learn about some of the inventions that helped shape the history and character of our country. You will see how progress in such fields as science, industry, medicine, transportation, and electronics made America strong and gave its people the highest standard of living in the world. Although the book mentions some inventors from other nations, its focus is on discoveries and inventions that took place within the United States itself.

Each chapter concludes with several pages of activities designed to challenge and motivate. Answers are provided in the Answer Key.

Everyday Life: Inventions provides a valuable supplement to any classroom textbook on American history.

Editor's note: Wherever applicable in the worksheets, metric equivalents have been given alongside the U.S. Customary measurement system. You may use either measurement system to work the problems. You also can try solving in one system and then try the other. Answers for both measurement systems are in the Answer Key.

The information in this book is as accurate as possible. Frequently sources did not agree on the most basic information, such as the inventor, the spelling of names, and the year of invention. We have provided the information we think to be accurate based on the best available evidence.

CHAPTER 1

New Implements Revolutionize Farming

During its early years, America was an agricultural nation. Tools and machinery were simple and basic, and not much changed until 1793. In that year, a tinkerer named Eli Whitney invented a machine that had a profound impact on American history.

The Cotton Gin

Thoughts of the South before the Civil War conjure up images of huge plantations worked by hundreds of slaves. This did occur in some places but came close to not happening at all.

For many years, cotton was not a profitable cash crop. It only grew in certain kinds of soil, and processing it was extremely slow. The problem lay in removing the seeds. It took one slave an entire day to clean one pound (.45 kilogram) of cotton. At this slow rate, conditions were unfavorable for the development of large plantations planted in acres and acres of cotton.

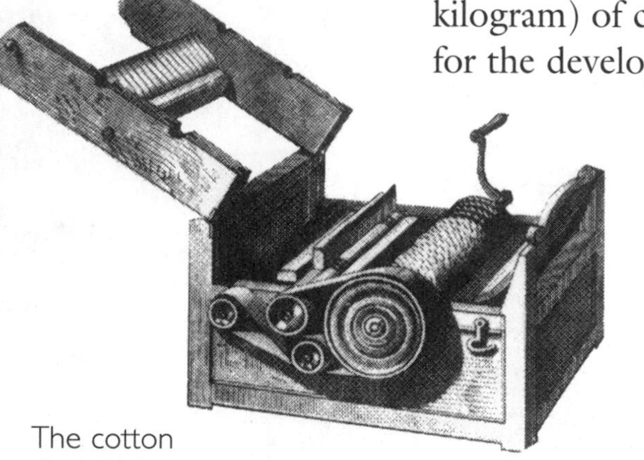

The cotton gin, which accelerated the process of removing the seeds from cotton, made increased acreage profitable and caused slavery to become even more entrenched in the South. From a drawing of an original gin.

What made the mass production of cotton possible was Eli Whitney's cotton gin. Whitney was the son of a Massachusetts farmer who grew up working with and repairing farm machinery. He worked his way through Yale University, and in 1793 set out for South Carolina to tutor the children of a wealthy planter. His plans fell through when another teacher was given the job. Then he met Catherine Greene, the widow of Revolutionary War hero General Nathanael Greene. Mrs. Greene invited young Whitney to stay as a guest at Mulberry Grove, her large plantation outside of Savannah, Georgia.

While at Mulberry Grove, Mrs. Greene, aware of Whitney's skill with machines, encouraged him to invent a device for removing the seeds from cotton. Whitney went to work at once, and in ten days he turned out the cotton gin. Within two years, his invention enabled the South to grow 8 million pounds (3.6 million kilograms) of cotton. This amount increased to 80 million pounds (36.3 million kilograms) twelve years later. Whitney's machine made the growing of cotton in vast amounts possible.

In spite of its benefits, the cotton gin had a negative effect on America's history. With more cotton being planted, there was a need for more slaves to

work on the plantations. Thus, Whitney's invention contributed largely to the strengthening and spread of slavery in the South.

The steel blade plow was a great advancement over those made of iron and wood. It made farming easier and helped increase production. From a photograph of an original John Deere plow.

The Steel Plow and the Reaper

Two inventions in 1834 made life easier and more profitable for the American farmer. The first was John Deere's steel plow. The second was Cyrus Hall McCormick's reaper.

Until the settlement of the American prairie, farmers tilled the soil with wooden and iron plows. These worked fine in normal types of soils. But the heavy grassy farmland of the prairie posed a problem. The wooden plow had difficulty penetrating the hard ground, and the sticky soil had a tendency to cling to both wooden and iron plows. John Deere, a New England blacksmith, made a model for a new plow out of an old circular saw. He found that soil did not stick to the steel surface, and a new plow was born.

Deere's steel plow made him a successful businessman. He opened a shop in Grand Detour, Illinois, and later a larger one in Moline, Illinois. In 1875, his factory turned out the first horse-drawn, riding plow. Deere's inventions enabled farmers to plant more seeds and therefore produce larger crops. The result was a tremendous increase in America's food supply.

Now that it was possible to grow more grain, a faster way had to be found to harvest it. McCormick found that way shortly after Deere's steel plow came into use.

For years, men had tried to make a reaper that cut wheat. More than forty people attempted and failed. Cyrus's own father had actually made a cutting machine, but it did not work very well. Farmers had to continue harvesting their crops with scythes and cradles.

Cyrus McCormick demonstrates his reaper before an enthusiastic crowd in 1831. From a famous 1930 painting.

Although Cyrus was a strong, young man, he did not like cutting wheat by hand any more than other farmers. One day he asked his father if he could work on his reaping machine and try to get it to cut better. The older McCormick concurred, and twenty-two-year-old Cyrus set to work. He soon had a machine that he felt would do the job. It was pulled by horses and featured four long blades that turned as the machine moved forward.

Cyrus demonstrated his reaper in a neighbor's field of oats. The weird-looking device caused quite a commotion among the local population. Farmers stared in disbelief as the noisy machine went about its task. Young boys shouted. Dogs barked. Doubters shook their heads. But the reaper worked! In just a few hours, it harvested as much grain as three men could cut by hand in a day.

The reaper made McCormick a rich man. He patented his device in 1834 and moved to Chicago. At the age of thirty-six, he opened a factory to produce harvesting machines. Because of his efforts, Chicago soon became the grain capital of the United States.

McCormick's reaper completely revolutionized farming in America. Larger farms that grew huge amounts of grain became a reality. In 1902, eighteen years after his death, McCormick's company joined with several others to form the present International Harvester Company.

Joseph Glidden's barbed wire enabled farmers to fence in their lands, ending the open range. From an advertisement lauding the virtues of barbed wire.

Barbed Wire

Even though the steel plow made farming practical on the Great Plains, one other invention was necessary for this large area to become permanently settled. That invention was barbed wire.

For a short time after the Civil War, the Great Plains was open-range cattle country. Wealthy cattle barons grazed their stocks on the unfenced lands, fattening them for shipment to the East. Anyone could drive and graze a herd anywhere without opposition.

The Homestead Act of 1862 changed this. The government promised to give 160 acres (65 hectares)of land to anyone who settled on it and cultivated it for five years. Soon large numbers of people flocked to the Plains. They felt they had as much right to the land as the cattle owners did.

In 1893, an Illinois farmer patented an invention that brought an end to the open range. Joseph Glidden's barbed wire gave farmers an inexpensive way to fence in land to keep cattle from destroying their crops. Glidden opened a factory in DeKalb, Illinois, that turned out 600 miles (965 kilometers) of barbed wire daily. With production so large, barbed wire was relatively cheap. Farmers began to fence in large tracts of the prairie, an act that infuriated the cattle owners. Cowboys responded by cutting the barbed wire. Soon range wars broke out between the homesteaders and those who favored an open range. The government supported the farmers, and the open range came to an end. Fencing off large areas of the Plains also brought an end to the American frontier. Having lost the struggle, cattle owners retreated to lands too dry for farming. In certain areas of the Southwest, they established some of the large cattle ranches that continue to this day.

Benjamin Hall came out with the first gasoline-powered tractor in 1904, but steam-driven tractors were used as early as 1890. This picture shows a cumbersome steam-driven tractor in use.

The Tractor

Farming entered the modern age with the invention of the tractor. Although it took many years, tractors eventually replaced horses and mules on most American farms.

The first tractors appeared in the 1890s. They were large, cumbersome machines powered by steam. Few farmers bought them because of their high price. A team of mules or horses could be purchased much more cheaply than the new mechanical devices.

In 1904, Benjamin Holt patented the first gasoline-powered tractor. It was a big improvement over its steam-driven predecessor. Holt's tractor was a crawler type, which meant that it moved on a belt or track similar to a tank. It was more maneuverable and easier to use than the steam-driven and animal-driven tractors. Still, farmers were slow to purchase it. It was cheaper to feed a horse or mule than to provide gasoline and oil for a tractor. There also were not many mechanics around in those days to keep the machines repaired and in the fields. It took more than fifty years for most farmers to discard the horse and mule in favor of the tractor. When they finally did, their productivity increased and their work was made considerably lighter.

Name ______________________________ Date ____________________

Solve Some Math

Complete using either the U.S. Customary or metric measurement system.

1. In 1792, two years before Eli Whitney invented the cotton gin, 138,000 pounds (62,597 kilograms) of Southern cotton were exported to England. By 1794, this number had increased to 1,600,000 pounds (725,760 kilograms).

   a. How many more pounds/kilograms of cotton were exported in 1794? __________ pounds/kilograms

   b. What percent increase in production took place between 1792 and 1794? Round to the nearest one.

   __________ %

2. Cotton is packed into bales weighing 500 pounds (227 kilograms) each. How many bales could have been packed from the 138,000 pounds (62,597 kilograms) of cotton exported in 1792? from the amount exported in 1794? Round to the nearest one.

   1792 __________ bales 1794 __________ bales

3. On a separate sheet of paper, make a line or bar graph of your own showing the amount of cotton picked in one week by each of the following workers on a plantation. (Use pounds for this exercise.)

   John—6 pounds

   James—6.5 pounds

   William—7 pounds

   Jesse—5.5 pounds

   Charles—5 pounds

   Robert—7.5 pounds

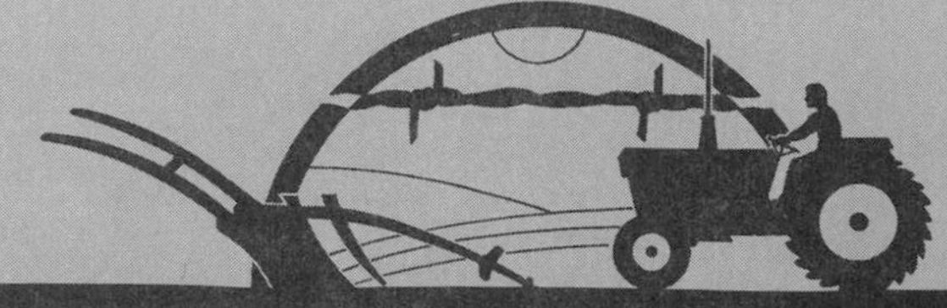

Name ______________________ *Date* ______________

Write a Letter to a Newspaper in the 1870s

You have learned that the invention of barbed wire led to the fencing-in of parts of the Great Plains that were previously open range. You will also recall that such acts led to bloody range wars between cattlemen and homesteaders, or farmers. Who, in your opinion, was justified in the actions they took?

Imagine yourself living in Nebraska in the 1870s at the height of the range wars. On the lines provided, write a letter to the editor of a newspaper supporting either the cattlemen or the homesteaders. In your letter, give reasons why you think the side you support is in the right.

Dear Editor:

Yours truly,

Name ______________________ *Date* ______________

Test Your Geography Skills

Both Eli Whitney, the inventor of the cotton gin, and John Deere, who invented the steel plow, were from New England.

New England is made up of six states. Locate these on a map or in an encyclopedia. Then write the names of the six states and their capitals on the lines at right.

State	Capitol
______________	______________
______________	______________
______________	______________
______________	______________
______________	______________
______________	______________

Look at a map of Massachusetts and answer the following questions:

1. Two states lie north of Massachusetts. They are ______________ and ______________ .
2. West of Massachusetts is the state of ______________ .
3. Two states that border Massachusetts to the south are ______________ and ______________.
4. ______________ is the capital of Massachusetts.

Cyrus McCormick, the inventor of the reaper, was born in Virginia. Look at a map of Virginia and answer the questions below.

1. The states of ______________ and ______________ border Virginia to the south.
2. If you lived in Richmond, Virginia, in which direction would you have to travel to visit a friend in Kentucky?

   ____

Name ______________________ Date ______________________

Debate the Use of Tractors

When the gasoline-powered tractor was patented in 1904, farmers were slow to embrace it. As you learned in this chapter, it took many years before most American farmers were ready to give up their horses and mules.

On the lines, create a dialogue (conversation) between Farmer A and Farmer B concerning the appearance of the tractor. Have one farmer support changing over to the new machine and the other argue in favor of the continued use of draft animals. Each farmer should give reasons why he feels the way he does.

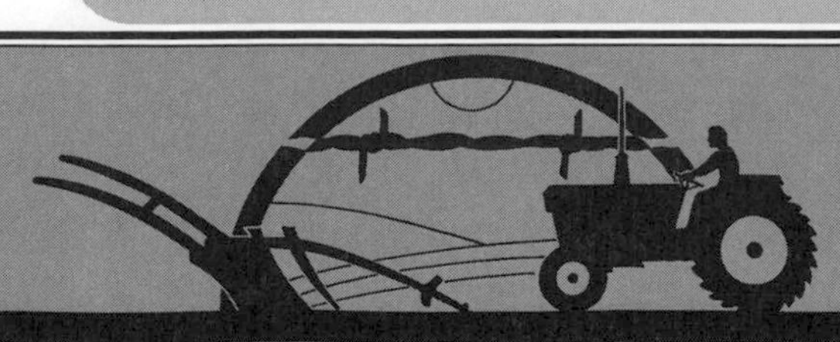

CHAPTER 2

Advances Are Made in Transportation

Man for centuries has dreamed of and experimented with new means of transportation. Leonardo da Vinci drew sketches of helicopters and parachutes as early as the fifteenth century. The French inventor Denis Papin envisioned a boat propelled by steam in the late 1600s. And numerous scientists and tinkerers began experimenting with a horseless carriage as far back as 1769.

The *Clermont* on its maiden trip between Albany and New York City on August 17, 1807. From a colored lithograph.

Few developments in modern transportation were the work of a single person. Most inventions came about through the contributions of many people over a period of time. The individual who received credit for a new idea was usually the one who made the first practical use of it.

The Steamboat

The first significant improvement in transportation was the steamboat. Its development occurred gradually over a period of more than a century. No fewer than fifty men either sought patents for the steamboat or laid claim to its invention. Two rival American claimants—John Fitch and James Rumsey—even came close to blows on a Philadelphia street while arguing about a patent.

But Robert Fulton is the inventor generally recognized as the steamboat's creator. His craft was the first practical version to be produced. It was also the first to become a commercial success.

As a youth, Fulton became an apprentice to a jeweler in Philadelphia. He became quite skilled as a painter of miniature portraits and seemed destined for a career in art. But his real interest lay in science and engineering. Soon he started devoting most of his time to scientific pursuits and only painted for amusement.

Fulton had a wide range of mechanical curiosity and ability. Before he built his steamboat, the *Clermont,* he designed an improved dredging machine for digging canals. He also made a submarine that managed to stay underwater for six hours.

Robert R. Livingston, America's ambassador to France, had a keen interest in the possibility of a boat that was run by steam. He promised to put up the money if Fulton would take on such a project. Fulton agreed and began work in 1802. By August 1807, he had the *Clermont* ready for its trial run from New York City to Albany.

On the morning of August 17, 1807, a group of distinguished ladies and gentlemen boarded the boat for its experimental trip up the Hudson River. As it chugged along at 5 miles (8 kilometers) an hour, crowds along the banks laughed and shouted. They called the smoking craft "Fulton's Folly." Some said that it looked like a sawmill on fire. But to everyone's surprise, the *Clermont* successfully made the 150-mile (241-kilometer) trip in thirty-two hours. A new era in transportation had begun.

Fulton's boat gave Americans a quick and easy way to travel from one city to another. In a few years, passenger steamships were sailing up and down rivers as far west as the Mississippi. They also ferried travelers across the Atlantic between America and Europe.

The Airplane

At about the same time that the steamboat became a reality, an Englishman produced a machine that revolutionized travel by land. Richard Trevithick, an inventor and engineer, invented the steam locomotive in 1804. In less than thirty years, trains were carrying passengers in both Europe and America. The locomotive, though not

The Wright brothers successfully test their airplane at Kitty Hawk, North Carolina, on December 17, 1903. Their first flight lasted 12 seconds.

an American invention, helped link the eastern and western parts of the United States shortly after the Civil War.

The next significant American contribution in transportation came almost 100 years after Fulton's steamboat. In 1903, Wilbur and Orville Wright made the first successful airplane flight at Kitty Hawk, North Carolina. Their success ended centuries of human frustration from attempts to fly.

Wilbur and Orville Wright were born in Dayton, Ohio. Their interest in flying began at an early age when their father bought them a toy helicopter. They marveled at the way it was propelled through the air by rubber bands. Soon they were reading everything they could find about early attempts at flying. They even read books on birds, studying how birds' wings made it possible for them to stay in the air.

For a while, Wilbur and Orville operated a bicycle repair shop in Dayton. The bicycle was a relatively new means of transportation, and there was much demand for the Wright brothers' services. Their business was so successful that they were able to devote some time to their lifelong interest: flying.

The brothers began by experimenting with box kites. They built various kinds in their attempt to find the one that performed best. Then they constructed a glider. People had tried to fly gliders for years, and a number had died in the process. Where others had failed, Wilbur and Orville were determined to succeed.

The Wrights needed an open, isolated place to test their glider. They chose the white sands along the Atlantic Ocean near Kitty Hawk, North Carolina. There, in the fall of 1900, they took turns gliding off an elevated area called Kill Devil Hill. Neither brother, however, was able to satisfactorily control the craft. After many attempts, they knew more study and experimentation were needed. And more money. The first glider had cost them only $15 to make!

Wilbur and Orville built two more gliders. These they tested with better results in 1901 and 1902. By 1903, they were ready to add an engine. After much planning, they designed and built a 4-cylinder, 12-horsepower gasoline motor that they hoped would lift the plane off the ground by means of two large propellers.

The Wrights chose December 17, 1903, to try the first powered-flight in history. They invited the people of Kitty Hawk to watch. Only two showed up, primarily because it was a cold, dismal day. As Wilbur and three employees from the Kitty Hawk Life Saving Station stood by nervously, Orville started

the engine and actually took off! He flew the strange-looking craft a total of 120 feet (36.6 meters). His flight lasted all of twelve seconds. But he had written a new page in history. The age of the airplane was born.

Wilbur and Orville Wright took turns flying their machine that day. Each time they improved on their previous performance.

In a matter of years, the airplane had seemingly shrunk the size of the United States. Coast-to-coast flights became commonplace. Mail and goods were sent across the country in record time. And by 1947, most places in the world were within reach in thirty or forty hours. Today, the airplane has truly made the world a global community.

Henry Ford's first car. Powered by a two-cylinder engine, it could attain the breath-taking speed of 10 miles (16 meters) an hour. Its wheels resembled those of a bicycle.

The Automobile

The gasoline-powered automobile, or "horseless carriage" as it was first called, was not an American invention. But it was an American who made it practical and affordable. That American was Henry Ford. He introduced the moving assembly line, making it possible to build large numbers of automobiles that could be sold at lower prices. His vehicles were within the price range of the average working family.

Henry Ford was born and raised on a farm near Dearborn, Michigan. But he was never really interested in farming. His burning passion was machines. He spent a good part of his time tinkering with the steam-powered implements on his father's farm. At the age of sixteen, he went to Detroit and became an apprentice machinist. Soon he was chief engineer at the Edison Illuminating Company in Detroit.

Ford began experimenting with gasoline engines in 1890. With the help of his wife Clara, he often worked and experimented in the kitchen of his home. He completed his first workable engine in 1893, and three years later built his first automobile.

In 1903, Ford started the Ford Motor Company. In the first year, he sold over 1,700 Model A Fords, as his first automobile was called. It sold for $850.

Workers assemble parts on one of Henry Ford's Model Ts at the Ford Motor Company in Highland Park, Michigan.

Five years later, Ford produced the Model T, which became the most popular car ever made in America. Admiring consumers called it the "Tin Lizzie." Its price was $550. By 1924, Ford had sold 2,000,000 Tin Lizzies, and the price had been lowered to $250. From 1908 to 1929, more than 15,000,000 Model T automobiles were traveling the roads of America. The Model T far outsold any of its competitors in the automobile market.

Henry Ford introduced the assembly line at his plant in 1913. Up until that time, it took workers several days to finish building one automobile. They had to move from one car to the next to install parts. In the process, they got in each other's way, and it took a lot of time to get anything accomplished. With the assembly line, each worker stood in one place and the automobile came to the worker on a conveyor belt. He had but one part to attach to the vehicle; when he completed his task, the car moved on to the next worker who added his part. This continued until the automobile was completely assembled. The assembly line enabled Ford to produce as many as 9,000 automobiles in one day.

Ford's new methods saved time and money. As a result, he was able to increase the wages of his skilled workers to $5 a day. This was unheard of at the time. In the early 1900s, the average skilled worker earned about $0.30 an hour, or $2.40 a day. Ford's increase more than doubled the salary of his employees.

The automobile had a profound effect on America. People no longer had to depend solely on trains and boats, whose schedules were seldom the same as theirs. The automobile led to the growth of suburbs. It was no longer necessary for workers to live in cities where they were close to their place of employment. The car allowed them to live outside the city and commute to work. Finally, the automobile stimulated the growth of other industries. Companies that produced steel, gasoline, and the many parts necessary to assemble automobiles flourished.

Name ______________________________ *Date* ____________________

Solve a Steamboat Puzzle

Fill in the sentences at the bottom of the page and complete each word in the puzzle at right. The sentences are based on the reading.

```
    _ _ _ S _ _
      _ _ T _ _
    _ _ _ E
          A _ _ _ _ _
  _ _ _ _ M _ _ _
      _ _ B _ _ _ _ _ _
        _ O _ _ _
    _ _ _ A _
    _ _ _ T _ _
```

1. The ______________________ River was the site of the first steamboat trip.
2. John ______________________ was one of the men who claimed to have invented the steamboat.
3. The *Clermont* traveled at a speed of ________ miles per hour.
4. The *Clermont*'s first trip was from New York City to ______________________________________.
5. Robert Fulton named his steamboat the ______________________________________.
6. Robert Fulton built an underwater boat called a ______________________________________.
7. People called the *Clermont* Fulton's ______________________.
8. The *Clermont* was powered by ______________________.
9. Robert ______________________________ invented the steamboat.

Name ______________________________ Date ____________________

Write a Newspaper Story

In 1896, one of the first automobiles built in America led a circus into a small town. People standing on the streets laughed and pointed. The automobile, like the steamboat earlier, was a novelty that few people thought would catch on with the public.

The first automobiles were slow and unreliable. Daredevils in horse-drawn carriages often challenged them to races. Sometimes the automobile won. At other times, the horse emerged the victor.

On the lines at right, create a short newspaper story about such a race. You can determine the outcome yourself. At the top, write a headline for your story and your byline (name).

The Daily Star

★★★★★★★★★★★★★★★★★

____

(Your headline)

by ______________________________

(Your name)

____

____

____

____

____

____

____

____

____

____

____

____

____

____

____

____

____

____

____

Name ______________________________ Date ____________________

Research and Make a Sketch

In this exercise, research and then draw and color a sketch of one of the following:

1. Robert Fulton's *Clermont*
2. The Wright brothers' airplane
3. Henry Ford's Model T

Name ______________________________ Date ____________________

Test Your Math Skills

Complete using either the U.S. Customary or metric measurement system.

1. The *Clermont* made the 150-mile (241-kilometer) trip from New York City to Albany in 32 hours. This was an average speed of ________ mph (kph).

2. In 1900, there were 4,000 automobiles sold in America. This number rose to 2,000,000 in 1920. How many more automobiles were sold in 1920 than in 1900?
   ____________ more

3. Create a word problem of your own using the information below. Space is provided at the bottom of the page for you to work your problem.

   In 1908 a Model T sold for $850. By 1924, the price was reduced to $250. In 1997, you could buy a new car for $12,000.

Name ______________________________ Date ____________________

Use Context Clues to Complete Sentences

Fill in the blanks in the sentences using the words below.

- aloft
- engine
- service
- transatlantic
- attached
- feat
- speed
- workhorse
- built
- hours
- still
- cause
- jointly
- successful
- distance
- passengers
- traveled

Five Historic Airplanes

On December 17, 1903, Wilbur and Orville Wright made the first ____________ airplane flights in history. Having _______________ a small, gasoline _____________ to their glider, the *Flyer,* each in turn soared into the sky from the beach at Kitty Hawk, North Carolina. Orville Wright took the controls first, and he kept the plane ______________________________ for twelve seconds and flew a __________________________ of 120 feet (about 37 meters).

By the end of the First World War, the airplane had come a long way. Charles Lindbergh further advanced its __________________ with a remarkable ________________ in May 1927. All alone in his monoplane, *The Spirit of St. Louis,* he made the first _____________ flight from New York to Paris in thirty-three __________________.

The _______________ of early commercial aviation was the DC-3, ______________ by the Douglas Aircraft Company. It carried thirty ________________ at a ________________ of 180 miles (290 kilometers) an hour. Some DC-3s are _____________ in use today.

A huge jump from the DC-3 was the British De Haviland Comet, the world's first jet airliner. It went into ________________ in 1952 and ___________________ at a speed of almost 500 miles (about 800 kilometers) an hour.

Today, the fastest commercial airliner is the Concorde SST. Built _________________ by France and Great Britain, it flies at a speed of 1,500 miles (about 2,400 kilometers) an hour.

CHAPTER 3

Communication Becomes Faster and Easier

For hundreds of years, people had no way of sending messages quickly from one place to another. Various methods were used, ranging from drums to flags and smoke signals. Even the Pony Express required several days to send news across the country. Then, in 1844, a miraculous event took place.

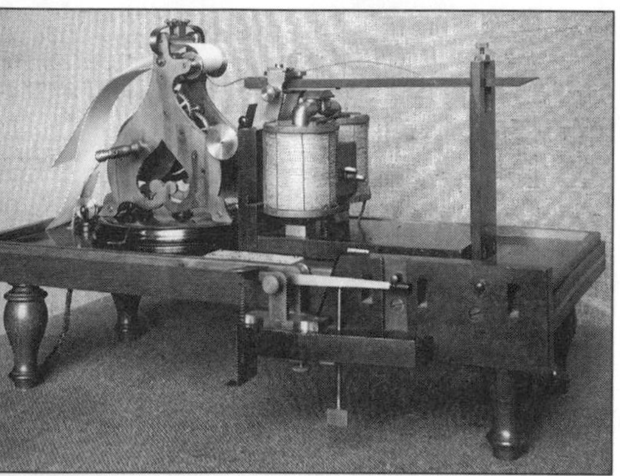

Samuel Morse's telegraph of 1837. The telegraph made it possible to send a message across the country in a matter of minutes.

The Telegraph

One day in the spring of 1844, an important message arrived in Washington, D.C. It announced that James K. Polk of Tennessee had been nominated for President by the Democratic Party at their national convention in Baltimore. The message had reached the nation's capital in a matter of minutes. How, people asked, could news travel 37 miles (59.5 kilometers) in such a short time?

The answer was the telegraph. The message sent on that day was the first important use of this new invention by Samuel F. B. Morse. It also marked the beginning of the age of modern communication. The appearance of the telegraph eventually led to the invention of radio and television.

Samuel Morse was a brilliant child who finished high school at the age of fourteen. He then entered Yale University to study art. From the start, however, he seemed torn between a career as an artist and that of a scientist. But art won out, and in 1811, his parents sent him to London to study. Four years later, he won recognition as an accomplished portrait painter.

Morse never earned a lot of money as an artist. He struggled just to make ends meet. But he did win acclaim in the United States for his artistic talent. Two of his portraits of Revolutionary War hero the Marquis de Lafayette hang today in New York City. One is at the New York Public Library; the other is at City Hall.

Morse's brief career as an artist took him to Europe on several occasions. It was while returning home from one trip in 1829 that he got the idea for the telegraph. Listening to a shipboard conversation one day, he heard several men discussing a discovery made by a scientist named Joseph Henry. Henry had invented an electric magnet that produced a spark. This gave Morse the idea for a machine that would send a message along a wire.

Several years passed before Morse started to work on his message-sending project. When he did, he ran half a mile of wire around his room and began experimenting. His idea was simple enough. Using a battery, he sent a charge of electricity through a wire. When the electricity reached the other end, it magnetized a piece of iron that Morse had wound around with the wire. Opening and closing an electrical circuit controlled the charge sent over the line. Electricity traveled through the wire when the circuit was closed but none went through when it was open. A key was used to open and close the circuit. Holding the key down for a long time created a long click, or "dash." A short click created a "dot." The dots and dashes were used in different combinations to form the letters of the alphabet. This method of sending messages over a wire became the famous Morse code.

In 1843, Morse received funding from Congress to run a telegraph line between Baltimore, Maryland, and Washington, D.C. His invention was an immediate success. In a matter of a few years, wires connected the main cities of most nations. In time, wireless telegraphy came into use.

In the 1920s the teletype replaced dot-and-dash messages. With the teletype, messages are typed into a teleprinter that resembles a typewriter. Then the message automatically types on a teleprinter in another city.

Lillian Sholes, daughter of the inventor of the typewriter, uses a working model of her father's machine in 1872. It went on the market the following year.

The Typewriter

About twenty-five years after the telegraph was invented, another device appeared that further improved the communication process. That device was the typewriter.

An English engineer named Henry Mill patented the first typewriter in 1714. But it was a clumsy apparatus and did not perform well. The first practical typing machine came on the scene in 1867. It was developed by three Milwaukee men: Christopher Latham Sholes, Carlos Glidden, and Samuel Soule. Sholes received a patent for the invention a year later. It was manufactured and put on the market in 1870 by E. Remington and Sons of Ilion, New York. (Remington and Sons also made guns.)

The typewriter worked by the force of the fingers striking several rows of keys. Each key represented a letter, number, or mark. Each key had an arm that lifted it to strike a ribbon soaked with ink. This printed the image of the letter on a piece of paper that was inserted between the ribbon and a rubber cylinder called a platen.

The first typewriter had two sets of type bars. One set was for capital letters and the other for lower-case letters. Later, both letters were put on one key and the typist typed a capital letter by pressing down on a shift key. Other features were added that made the typewriter a more practical machine. Two of these were the margin release and the backspace lever. Another was a bell that warned the typist when the end of a line was near.

The first typewriters were large and cumbersome. You have probably seen examples of these at flea markets and antique stores. As time went on, typewriters became smaller and more streamlined.

In the 1920s the first electric typewriters were introduced. They considerably reduced the level of noise caused by the keys and were much easier to use.

A further advancement was the portable typewriter. It quickly became popular with students, writers, and business people whose jobs required a considerable amount of travel.

Alexander Graham Bell makes the first long-distance call from New York to Chicago in 1892. He had invented the telephone sixteen years earlier.

Today, the typewriter is slowly going the way of the dinosaur. Many people who once relied on typewriters now use computers. But for almost a century, the typewriter was an invaluable tool in speeding up the process of correspondence and letter-writing.

The Telephone

Samuel Morse's telegraph made scientists everywhere wonder if the human voice could be sent over a wire. A German scientist, Philip Reis, had actually transmitted musical notes over a wire for a short distance in 1860. It was only a matter of time before someone discovered how to relay speech in the same way.

It is interesting to note that the transmission of the human voice over a wire was accomplished by someone who was actually trying to develop an improved hearing aid. Alexander Graham Bell was a teacher for the hearing impaired in Boston, Massachusetts. In 1877, he married one of his former hearing impaired students, a woman named Mabel Hubbard. It was his love for her that motivated him to work on a better hearing device. Mabel's father, wealthy Bostonian attorney Gardiner Hubbard, provided the funds for Bell to continue his experiments with sound. While working on the hearing aid, Bell stumbled upon the principles of the telephone.

With Gardiner Hubbard's financial backing, Bell was able to hire an assistant, Thomas Watson. The two carried out experiments in the attic of a Boston boardinghouse. They sometimes made so much noise that the landlady threatened to evict them.

Bell had to solve two problems before the telephone became a reality. The first was to send several messages over a telegraph wire at the same time. The second was to send an electric current that could be made to vary in strength. He solved both problems in March 1876.

One day Bell and Watson were in different rooms in the attic of the boardinghouse. They were preparing to try out a new transmitter that Bell had made. Suddenly, Bell spilled battery acid on his trousers. Alarmed, he shouted "Mr. Watson, come here, I want you!" Watson rushed excitedly through the door, informing Bell that he had heard his voice through the receiver in the other room. Bell then knew he had succeeded: It was possible to send the human voice through a wire. In his excitement, he forgot all about the acid that had ruined his clothes.

Bell's father-in-law founded the Bell Telephone Company in 1877. The following year, the first telephone exchange opened in New Haven, Connecticut. In 1892, Bell himself made the first long-distance call from New York to Chicago. This was followed twenty-three years later by the first telephone conversation to be transmitted coast-to-coast. Finally, in 1923, the first overseas call took place between New York and England. Like the airplane, the telephone helped bring the world closer together.

Bell's invention was also a boon to business. It stimulated the economy and gave jobs to thousands of people, especially women. Many women became switchboard operators as more and more telephone exchanges opened throughout America.

Name ______________________ *Date* ______________

Convert Scores to Morse Code

Imagine you are a ham radio operator sending Friday's baseball scores to a friend in another part of the world. To do so, you would use the code devised by Samuel F. B. Morse when he invented the telegraph in 1843.

Look up the Morse code in an encyclopedia or some other book. Then, on the lines provided beside the results of the following games, write in dots and dashes showing how you would transmit the scores. You need only concern yourself with the symbols for numbers.

1. Indians 2 Yankees 1 — Indians ______ Yankees ______
2. Red Sox 8 Blue Jays 3 — Red Sox ______ Blue Jays ______
3. Dodgers 4 Padres 0 — Dodgers ______ Padres ______
4. Athletics 6 Mariners 2 — Athletics ______ Mariners ______
5. Rangers 5 White Sox 4 — Rangers ______ White Sox ______
6. Braves 1 Reds 0 — Braves ______ Reds ______
7. Cubs 7 Marlins 2 — Cubs ______ Marlins ______
8. Mets 9 Phillies 3 — Mets ______ Phillies ______
9. Orioles 4 Tigers 1 — Orioles ______ Tigers ______
10. Astros 3 Cardinals 0 — Astros ______ Cardinals ______

After sending the scores, you need to sign off. On the line below, write how you would send your name in Morse code.

____

Name ______________________ Date ______________________

Test Your Vocabulary Using Context

The meaning of a word often depends on its context, or the way it is used in a sentence.

How good are you at using context clues to better understand what you have read? Try your skills on the narrative at right.

Fill in the blanks in the sentences using these words.

- business
- laborious
- practical
- combined
- manufacturers
- price
- communicative
- Milwaukee
- produced
- expensive
- patent
- replaced
- handwritten
- popular
- typewriters

You have learned that the first ______________________ typewriter was developed by three men from ______________. One of them, Christopher Latham Sholes, was issued a ______________________ for the invention in 1868.

Before the typewriter, all correspondence was ______________. This was a ______________________ process that required much time and patience. The typewriter did away with this drudgery and improved the ______________________ process.

The first ______________________ were large and cumbersome. They were also ______________________. They sold for about $125, which in those days was a lot of money. Gradually, as more of the machines were ______________________, the ______________________ came down. As the typewriter became ______________________, more and more companies made them. In 1909, there were eighty-nine typewriters ______________________ in the United States. Most of these later ______________________ with other companies or went out of ______________________.

Typewriters today have largely been ______________________ by computers.

Name ______________________ Date ______________

Rewrite History

Imagine some event in history turning out in a way other than it did. (For example, what would the world be like today if the Axis Powers had won World War II?)

Thinking along these lines, suppose that such communication devices as the telegraph and telephone had never been invented. Or that radio and television had never come about. How would America be different today? What about the world?

On the lines, write how you think history might have turned out differently without these advancements.

Name ______________________________ Date ____________________

Use a Bar Graph to Compare Facts

One year after the Bell Telephone Company was formed, there were 10,755 telephones in use in America. Compare this with 7.6 million by 1910! As you can see, the number of telephones in service increased dramatically in a few short years.

The largest increase in the number of telephones in the United States occurred in the 1950s. By 1955, 60 percent of American homes had telephones. This meant there were about 53 million in use at that time.

The bar graph shows the comparatively low number of telephones in use in other countries in 1955.

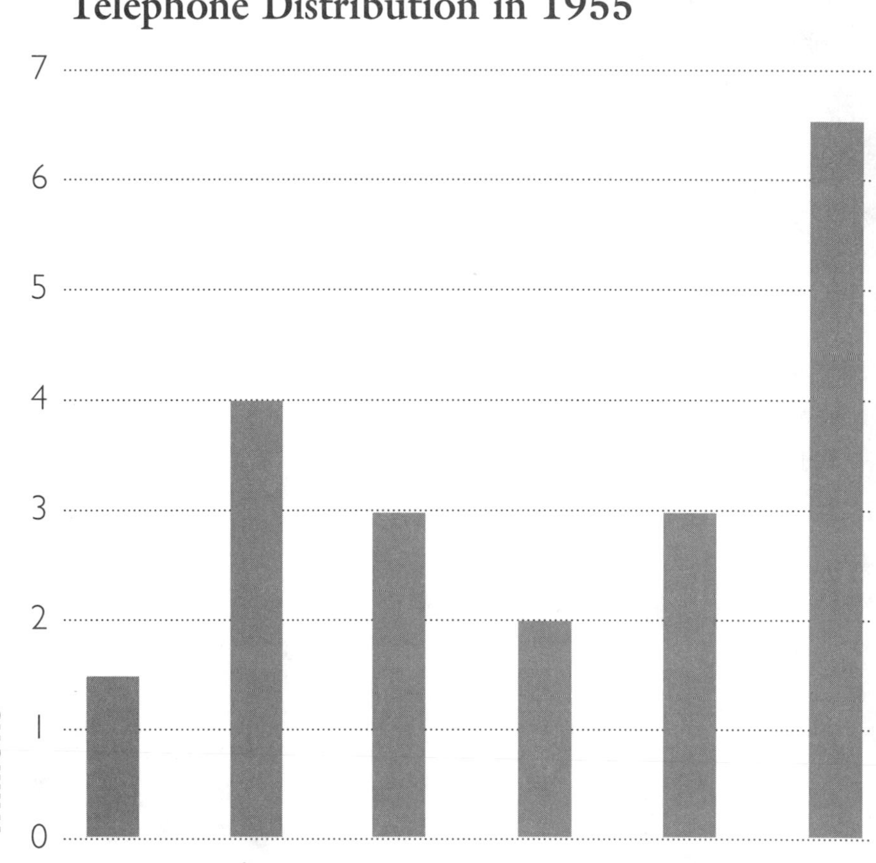

Use the graph to answer the questions below.

1. The total number of telephones in the six countries included on the graph was __________.
2. How many more telephones did the United Kingdom have than Italy? __________
3. Which country had the least number of telephones?

   ____
4. The United Kingdom had about __________ times as many telephones as Canada (round to nearest whole number).

Name ______________________________ *Date* ____________________

Create a Simple String Telephone

Imagine the excitement shared by Alexander Graham Bell and Thomas Watson when they first heard their voices over the telephone.

You can experience some of that excitement yourself by making a string telephone. Not only will it help you better understand how sound vibrations travel, it will also be fun.

Here is what you need:

1. a piece of string or thin wire about 20 feet (6 meters) in length
2. 2 five-ounce (about 150 milliliters) paper cups (the kind used in kitchen paper-cup dispensers)
3. a pin
4. 2 small pieces of transparent tape

Here is what you do:

1. Make a pinhole in the bottom of each paper cup.
2. Push one end of the string or wire through the hole in each cup. Leave enough string to tie knots. Tape the knots to the inside of each cup.
3. Your "telephone" is now ready to use. Ask a friend or family member to take one end of the telephone into another room. By holding the string or wire taut, you should be able to talk to each other. Talk into the cup when you want to communicate, and hold it to your ear when you want to hear what the other person is saying.

Have fun!

CHAPTER 4

Medical Discoveries Improve Our Health

Picture an operating table at some point during the centuries before the mid-1800s. Four strong men struggle to hold a patient still while a "doctor" performs surgery. If the operation is taking place in a large city, the surgeon might have the drug opium to ease the patient's pain. If opium is unavailable, the unfortunate person on the table has probably been given a considerable amount of rum (or other liquor) to drink before the ordeal begins, which only slightly lessens the pain. If the scene happens to be occurring somewhere on the frontier, probably neither rum nor opium are on hand. In that case, a bullet or stick is placed between the patient's teeth for him or her to bite down on, and the doctor goes about his unpleasant task.

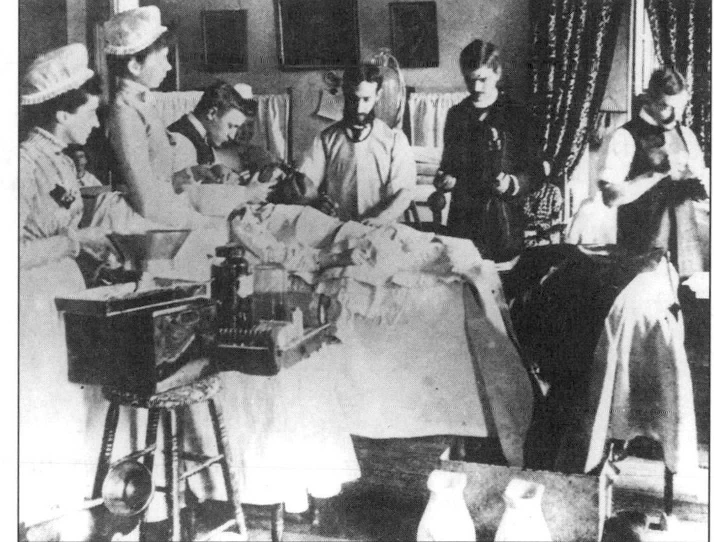

A man undergoes surgery in his home in the late 1800s. By that time, ether had come into wide use as an anesthetic. It was usually administered by holding a sponge soaked in the liquid over the patient's nose.

Ether

Surgery was a traumatic experience in America and elsewhere for many years. There were few certified doctors and no real means of anesthesia. Then, in 1842, a discovery appeared that made surgery bearable for the patient. That discovery was ether.

Ether is a liquid produced by the action of sulfuric acid on ethyl alcohol. Breathing its fumes can cause a person to lose consciousness. It was first used in an operation by Dr. Crawford W. Long of Jefferson, Georgia. Long gave ether to a patient who had a neck tumor. The patient fell into a deep sleep and felt no pain as the tumor was removed.

Dr. Long did not publish his findings or procedures at the time, and his discovery, therefore, received no publicity. Soon other doctors discovered and began using ether, and there was a controversy as to its real first discoverer. Historians, however, generally give credit to Dr. Long.

The discovery and use of ether was a huge step in the progress of medicine. Overnight it ended the nightmare of pain during surgery. It also made possible long and difficult operations that doctors previously would never have attempted.

The iron lung saved the lives of thousands of polio victims. Before its development in 1928, many people stricken with polio died because of paralysis of the muscles and organs of breathing.

The Iron Lung

It was 1928 before America made another significant contribution to medicine. That contribution came in the form of a device that saved thousands of people who had been stricken with polio.

Poliomyelitis, or polio as it is commonly called, is an acute viral infection. Viruses attack the nerve centers in the brain and the spinal cord, causing muscular paralysis. Because it is mainly a children's disease, polio is often called infantile paralysis.

But polio can also attack adults. Franklin Delano Roosevelt, our thirty-second President, contracted polio in 1921 at the age of thirty-nine. He was disabled the rest of his life. He died in 1945.

Some people with polio have difficulty breathing. The chest muscles become paralyzed and are unable to function properly. Until a way was found to help them breathe, many patients suffocated because they could not get enough air into their lungs.

In 1928, Philip Drinker and Louis A. Shaw found a solution to the problem. They developed the first iron lung, which assisted polio victims in breathing. The two Harvard doctors devised a large tank into which the patient was placed. Only the patient's head remained outside. A pump removed air from the tank, causing the patient's chest to expand and air to enter through the nose and mouth. When air was pumped back into the tank, the patient was able to exhale.

The iron lung saved thousands of polio victims from certain death. It was eventually replaced by a less cumbersome respirator. The respirator also helped patients who suffered from emphysema to breathe more easily.

Penicillin and Streptomycin

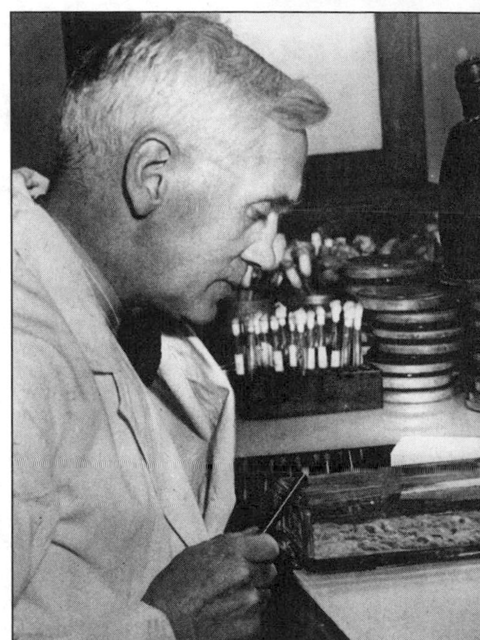

Sir Alexander Fleming, who discovered penicillin in 1928. The British bacteriologist gave the world its first effective way to treat bacteria-related diseases.

In the same year that the iron lung was invented, 1928, a British bacteriologist made a discovery that remains one of the greatest advancements in the history of medicine. Alexander Fleming, working at the University of London, accidentally discovered that a green mold called *penicillium notatum* stopped the growth of certain bacteria and prevented them from spreading. From his discovery came a new drug called penicillin. This marked the beginning of the era of antibiotics in the fight against bacteria-related diseases.

Fleming was not the first scientist to use the word *antibiotic*. The word is attributed to Selman A. Waksman, an American microbiologist at Rutgers University in New Brunswick, New Jersey. Waksman himself made important discoveries in the field of antibiotics.

Waksman was born in Kiev, Russia, in 1888. He came to the United States in 1910 to become a student at Rutgers. Eight years later he became a professor of microbiology at the same university, and shortly afterwards was promoted to department head. He carried on his experiments at the Agricultural Experiment Station of Rutgers.

Waksman's first major discovery was actinomycin, an antibiotic used to treat cancer. But he is most remembered for his discovery of streptomycin in 1944.

Streptomycin is an antibiotic made from a mold that grows in the soil. Waksman found it to be effective in treating illnesses that proved resistant to penicillin. Tuberculosis, meningitis, and urinary tract infections responded well to this new drug, as did endocarditis, a bacterial infection of the lining of the heart. For his discovery of streptomycin, Selman Waksman was awarded the Nobel Prize for Medicine in 1952.

The Polio Vaccine

The iron lung was the first effective way of preventing death among polio victims. But for twenty-five years after the iron lung's appearance, there was still no way of preventing the onset of polio. Thousands of people worldwide continued to die each year from the effects of this crippling disease.

In 1954, a miraculous vaccine was developed by Dr. Jonas E. Salk at the University of Pittsburgh. The vaccine could not have come at a more

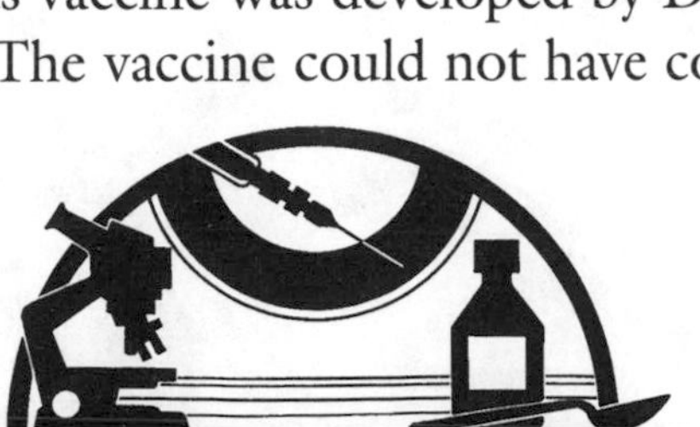

Dr. Jonas Salk, the University of Pittsburgh research scientist who developed a vaccine for polio in 1954. His discovery eventually led to polio being virtually eliminated in the Western Hemisphere.

opportune time. In the United States alone, more than thirty-eight thousand new cases of polio were reported the very year the vaccine was discovered.

Dr. Jonas Salk was a research scientist who originally planned to become a lawyer. Once in college, however, he became interested in science, particularly in viruses. He obtained his medical degree in 1939 from the New York University School of Medicine. Afterwards, he did research at the University of Michigan. While at Michigan, he helped develop an effective vaccine against influenza. In 1947, he transferred to the University of Pittsburgh. It was there that he made the discovery that brought him medical acclaim.

In his research, Salk identified three viruses that caused polio. He grew these in test tubes in his laboratory. He then killed the viruses with a formaldehyde solution and used them to make a vaccine. He knew he could not test the vaccine on humans right away, so he began by inoculating monkeys. None of the monkeys he injected with the vaccine contracted polio.

Satisfied with the results, Salk inoculated himself; his wife, Donna; and their three sons. The results were the same as with the monkeys. No one became ill because of the shots. Dr. Salk now knew he had found the way to prevent poliomyelitis.

In 1954, almost two million schoolchildren in the United States received the polio vaccine. The following year, the U.S. Public Health Service approved the manufacture of the vaccine for distribution throughout the country. The result was miraculous. The number of polio cases fell from 21,000 annually to just seven by 1974. Today, the disease has been completely eliminated in North, Central, and South America. The last reported incidence of polio in the Western Hemisphere was in Peru in 1991. Unfortunately, the disease is still prevalent in Africa and Asia.

Children in the United States receive the polio vaccine orally—at two months, four months, fifteen months, and, finally, between the ages of four and six prior to entering school.

Name ______________________________ Date ____________________

Write About Modern Medicine

In this chapter, you learned how the development of antibiotics and vaccines brought previously untreatable diseases under control.

Before the discovery of such wonder drugs, disease and epidemics killed hundreds of thousands. The bubonic plague of the fourteenth century killed from one-third to one-half of the population of Europe. An outbreak of influenza at the close of World War I killed an estimated twenty million people worldwide. More than 548,000 died in the United States alone. This was four times the number of American troops who lost their lives on the battlefield.

Today, some medical experts fear that the world is headed for a new "Middle Age" of medicine where disease and epidemics will once again kill thousands. The reason? These authorities point out that the overuse of antibiotics has resulted in certain viruses and bacteria becoming resistant to the antibiotics. It is true that such diseases as pneumonia and ear infections have become immune to certain drugs that once proved effective in their treatment. There are also new viruses and bacteria that have surfaced for which cures are yet to be found.

Create a dialogue between two doctors who are concerned about the reduced effectiveness of modern medicines. Continue on a separate sheet of paper.

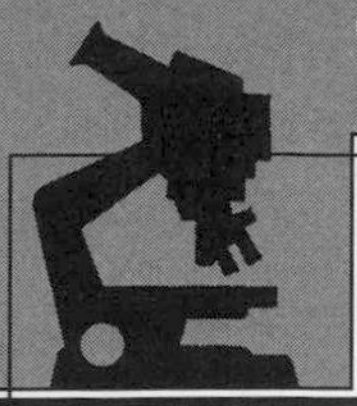

Name ______________________ Date ______________

Test Your Geography Knowledge

While working in Cuba with Dr. Walter Reed, the man who discovered the connection between yellow fever and mosquitoes, a young assistant decided to tour the Caribbean. Help him along the way by using the place names below to fill in the blanks in the sentences. Use a map of the Caribbean area to complete the exercise.

- Colombia
- Panama
- Costa Rica
- Port-au-Prince
- Dominican Republic
- Puerto Rico
- Haiti
- San Juan
- Havana
- Santo Domingo
- Hispaniola
- United States

Dr. Reed's assistant sailed southeast from Cuba, arriving at the large island of ______________________.

This island is divided into the nations of ______________________ and the ______________________. Their capitals are ______________ and ______________, respectively.

After leaving this first port of call, the young assistant continued to sail due east. He next came to the island of ______________, which is a part of the ______________________. Its capital is ______________________.

Before returning to Cuba, Dr. Reed's assistant decided he would like to see the Pacific Ocean. To do so, he had to pass through the ______________________ Canal. Upon his return, he stopped for brief visits in ______________________ and ______________, the countries on either side of Panama.

His journey completed, the doctor returned to ______________, the capital of Cuba.

Name ______________________________ Date ____________________

Rank the Discoveries

In this chapter you studied four important contributions made to medicine by American doctors and scientists. Which, in your opinion, was the most important? Which was the second in importance?

Rank these contributions 1 to 4 in the order of importance you assign them (1 being most important; 4 being least important).

_____ Iron lung

_____ Ether

_____ Polio vaccine

_____ Streptomycin

On the lines at right, explain why you ranked the discoveries the way you did.

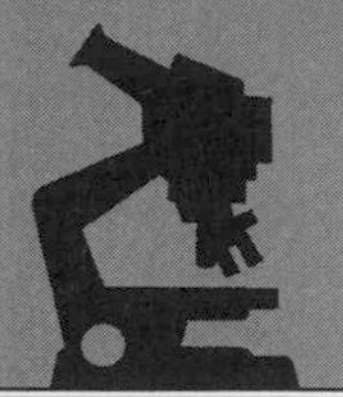

Name ______________________________ Date ____________________

Solve a Puzzle About Medicine

Across

1 Alexander Fleming discovered it

3 What the iron lung helped patients do

4 Infantile paralysis

5 Streptomycin is one

6 Carriers of yellow fever

10 Where Selman Waksman taught

11 Dr. Crawford Long first used it

12 He and Shaw developed the iron lung

Down

2 The ________ Prize for Medicine

4 Dr. Salk worked at this university

7 An operation by a medical doctor

8 Dr. Walter ________

9 He developed the polio vaccine

CHAPTER 5

New Weapons Change the Way Wars Are Fought

Until World War I, war was seen by some people as a glorious affair. Soldiers marched off to battle amid the fanfare of band music and tossed flowers. People felt that any war that started was sure to be over in a matter of weeks. No one was supposed to be killed, and everyone would return a hero.

World War I changed this naive concept of war. This first conflict to involve the entire world was the most destructive war in history. More than 14,000,000 people were killed and twice that number were maimed. When World War I finally ended after four terrible years, the world cried, "Never again." Yet, twenty years later, a second and even more destructive world war broke out. And World War II produced even more destructive weapons, the most powerful of which was the atomic bomb.

But we are far ahead of the story. To begin a survey of America's contributions to weaponry, we must go back more than 150 years.

The Submarine

John P. Holland of the United States developed the modern submarine in 1898. But the first attempt to use an underwater boat in warfare actually occurred during the Revolutionary War.

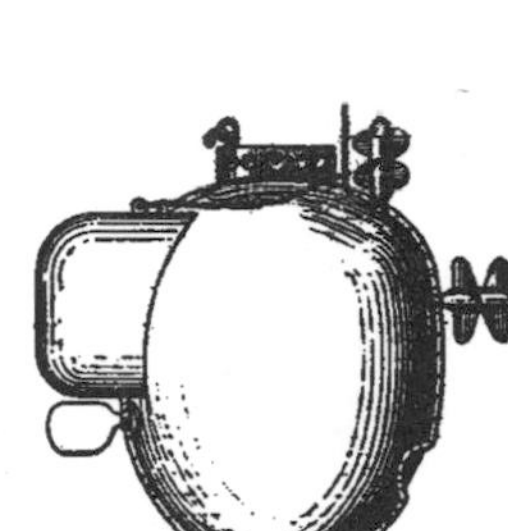

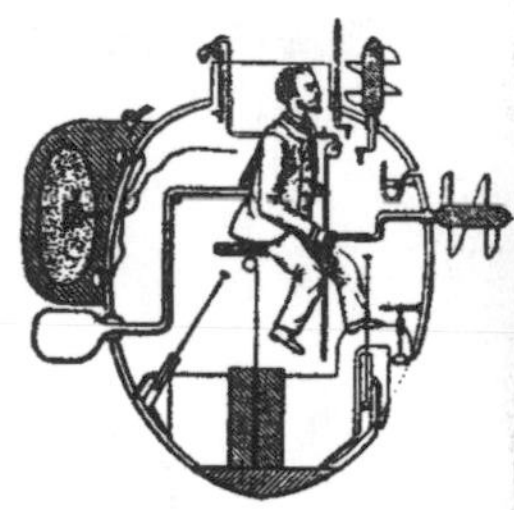

The world's first underwater boat, David Bushnell's hand-powered *Turtle*. It was actually used in an attempt to sink a British ship off Governors Island in 1776. The attack failed, but the enemy ship fled.

To call this early vessel a submarine might be stretching it. It looked more like a top, and bobbed like a cork. Invented by David Bushnell of Connecticut and christened the *Turtle*, it was used against the British in 1776.

The *Turtle* was a one-man sub powered by hand-cranked propellers. "Driven" by Sergeant Ezra Lee, it was equipped with two drill-like devices designed to plant a time bomb into a ship's hull. Like everything else on the *Turtle*, the drills were hand-cranked. Diagrams show Sergeant Lee even using his feet and elbows to operate and maneuver the vessel.

One night early in the war, the Turtle submerged and approached the British ship the H.M.S. *Eagle* off Governors Island in New York Harbor. Sergeant Lee guided the small submarine under the *Eagle*'s hull and commenced the attack. He drilled and drilled and drilled—all to no avail. The hulls of British ships were covered with copper to protect them from wood-eating worms. Unable to plant the bomb in the ship's hull, Lee turned the *Turtle* and fled. The bomb exploded harmlessly in the water, causing no damage to the enemy but almost capsizing the *Turtle*.

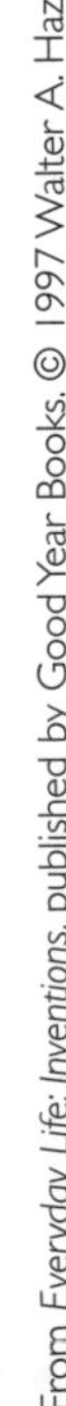

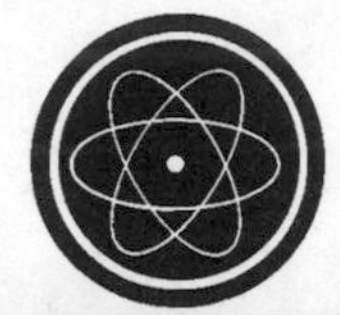

Although a failure, the attempted attack caused the British to move their ships to a safer harbor. The *Turtle* was proof that a submersible boat might one day play a role in the future history of naval warfare.

And indeed it did. From Bushnell's primitive *Turtle* to Holland's improved machine to today's nuclear-powered crafts, the submarine became a vital part of the war arsenal of many nations.

The Revolver

Lovers of Western films are familiar with the term "six-shooter." The six-shooter is a revolver that played a major role in the history of the American West.

A revolver is a pistol that has a cylinder with multiple chambers. Each chamber is leaded with a cartridge, or bullet. When the weapon is fired, the cylinder rotates, aligning the next chamber with the barrel. This rotating action enables the user to fire a number of bullets without having to reload.

The revolver was developed in 1835 by a twenty-one-year-old inventor named Samuel Colt. From his early teens, Colt was fascinated by guns and explosives. When he was fourteen, he devised an underwater mine of which he was very proud. He posted signs around town advertising his intent to blow a raft out of the water on the Fourth of July. Curious, a large crowd gathered to watch the demonstration at a pond in Ware, Connecticut.

Young Samuel beamed as he prepared to detonate his device. Unfortunately, he did not notice that the raft he planned to destroy had come loose and started drifting away from the charge. When he set off his mine, he blew a huge hole in the bottom of the pond. A mountain of muddy water sprayed the startled spectators, ruining their holiday clothes. Colt narrowly escaped harm at the hands of the angry crowd.

Colt was no more successful at Amherst Academy. He was constantly in trouble with school authorities because of his experiments. Once he even set part of the school on fire. Finally, the faculty requested that he leave, and, therefore, he never completed his studies.

After Amherst, at sixteen, young Colt joined the navy and went to sea. While sailing the Indian Ocean, he got the idea for the revolver by watching the helmsman maneuver the ship's steering wheel. He thought the same principle could be applied to a series of chambers that rotated around a cylinder. He carved a working model from a piece of wood. He was only a teenager, yet was well on his way to becoming an inventor.

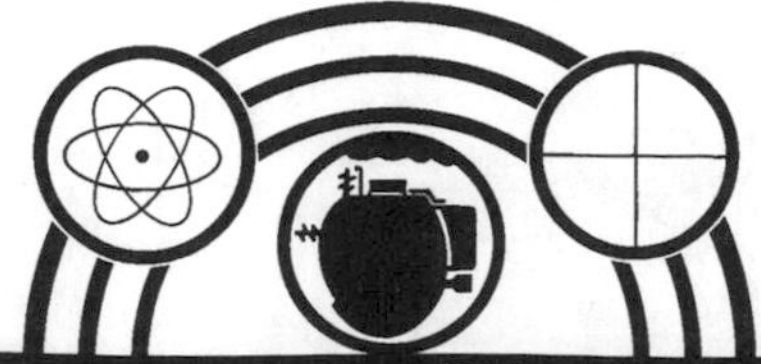

Colt received a patent for the revolver in 1836. In 1852, he opened a factory in Hartford, Connecticut, and began mass-producing the pistol. His handgun was later adopted and used by cowboys and soldiers throughout the West.

The Gatling Gun

Of the 14,000,000 soldiers who died in World War I, nine of every ten were killed by machine gun fire. The forerunner of the machine gun was the Gatling gun.

The Gatling gun was invented by Richard Gatling, the son of a North Carolina planter. Gatling invented his gun in a roundabout way. His first inventions were in agriculture, and he received several patents for farm machinery before his twenty-fifth birthday. When he was thirty-one, he went to medical school. But he never practiced medicine. His main interest always was in creating things. In 1862, he invented the gun for which he is remembered.

The Gatling gun, the forerunner of the modern machine gun, could fire 600 rounds a minute when a soldier turned its crank rapidly. The Gatling gun first saw action during the Civil War.

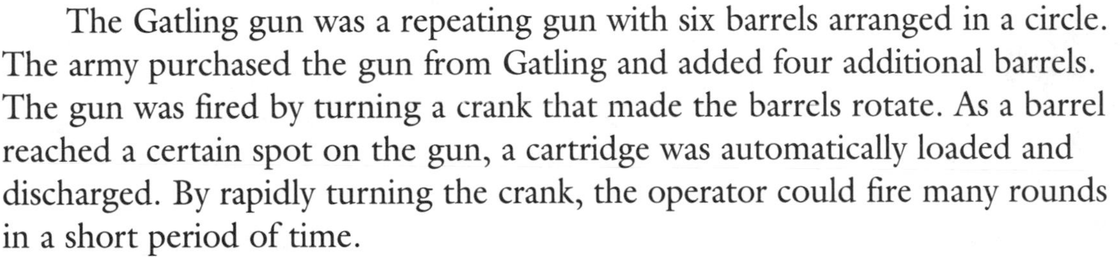

The Gatling gun was a repeating gun with six barrels arranged in a circle. The army purchased the gun from Gatling and added four additional barrels. The gun was fired by turning a crank that made the barrels rotate. As a barrel reached a certain spot on the gun, a cartridge was automatically loaded and discharged. By rapidly turning the crank, the operator could fire many rounds in a short period of time.

The U.S. Army bought Gatling's gun and used it on a limited basis during the Civil War. It was not used extensively, however, until the war with Spain in 1898. The Gatling gun was eventually replaced by the machine gun, invented in 1889 by Hiram S. Maxim of Great Britain.

The Atomic Bomb

Almost a century passed before America added another weapon to the world's growing arsenal. That weapon was the atomic bomb.

The atomic bomb was the most destructive device ever made. It was as powerful as 20,000 tons (18,140 metric tons) of dynamite. Besides the devastation caused by its blast, it created firestorms and radioactive fallout that added tremendously to its death toll.

The atomic bomb resulted from the theories of Albert Einstein, a German-born scientist. Einstein fled Nazi Germany in 1933 and came to the

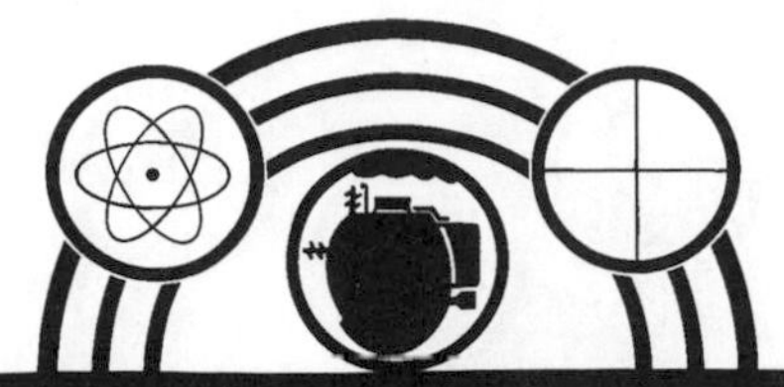

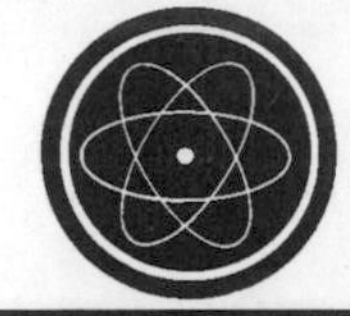

United States. He convinced President Franklin D. Roosevelt that such a bomb was possible.

Actual work on the atomic bomb took place in New Mexico. J. Robert Oppenheimer supervised the project, assisted by such well-known scientists as Enrico Fermi and Edward Teller. Work was carried out under tight security, and all employees associated with the bomb's making were sworn to secrecy.

The second atomic bomb to be dropped on Japan explodes over Nagasaki on August 9, 1945. Three days earlier, another atomic bomb had destroyed the city of Hiroshima.

Robert Oppenheimer did not know what to expect when the bomb was ready for testing. No one knew what would happen when countless atoms of uranium were split, causing the explosion. One scientist worried that the entire state of New Mexico might be wiped off the map. Another thought the world might be destroyed.

On July 16, 1945, the first atomic bomb was exploded in the desert near Alamogordo, New Mexico. It was a success. Three weeks later, on August 6, the bomb was dropped on Hiroshima, Japan. Although it killed 70,000 people, the Japanese government refused to surrender and end World War II. Three days later, a second bomb was dropped on the city of Nagasaki. It killed more than 35,000. The next day, the Japanese asked for peace.

Many people criticized President Harry Truman for using the atomic bomb against Japan. They claimed that the Japanese were close to surrendering and that the bomb was not necessary. Others supported the President. These supporters pointed out that, without the bomb, an invasion of Japan itself would be necessary to bring about peace. And such an invasion could possibly cause the deaths of 1,000,000 American soldiers.

The year 1945 marked the beginning of the atomic age. Seven years after Hiroshima and Nagasaki, an even more powerful weapon was tested for the first time. It was the hydrogen bomb. The hydrogen bomb was equal to 15,000,000 tons (13,605,000 metric tons) of dynamite. This made it seven hundred times more powerful than the atomic bomb.

Atomic weapons had far-reaching effects on the United States and the world. From 1945 onward, the fear of nuclear war was ever-present. To meet the threat, nations devoted more of their resources to national defense. The daily lives of citizens everywhere changed. People built bomb shelters, and schools conducted bomb drills in preparation for a possible nuclear attack.

The world was never the same after 1945.

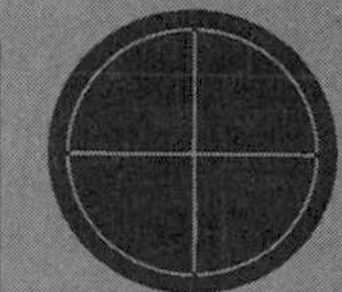

Name ________________________________ Date ______________________

Use Context Clues to Complete Sentences

Based on your reading in this chapter, fill in the blanks in the sentences using the words from the list below.

- capsizing
- hull
- pilot
- *Turtle*
- dates
- inventor
- planting
- underwater
- demonstrated
- laughed
- powered
- escape
- modern
- sink
- failed
- nation
- top

Some people may think the submarine is a ____________________ device associated with the twentieth century. But the submarine ____________________ back to the Revolutionary War, when a crude ____________________ boat was used against the British.

The boat in question was David Bushnell's ____________________. It was a small, one-person sub ____________________ by hand-cranked propellers. Colonists who saw it must have ____________________, because it looked more like a ____________________ than a weapon of war.

Sergeant Ezra Lee, the boat's ____________________, hoped to ____________________ a British ship by ____________________ a bomb in its ____________________. Unfortunately, Sergeant Lee could not penetrate the British ship's hull, and the plan ____________________. The bomb, however, went off as expected, almost ____________________ the *Turtle*. Sergeant Lee was lucky to ____________________ with his life.

No attempt was made to use another underwater boat in combat until the Civil War. But before that time, Robert Fulton, the ____________________ of the steamboat, built a submarine that he successfully ____________________ in 1800. Much to his dismay, however, no ____________________ showed any interest in it.

Name ____________________ Date ____________

Write a Letter to the Editor

No one denied that the atomic bomb was a terrible weapon of destruction. As the chapter points out, this bomb destroyed two Japanese cities and killed thousands of people. Many others died later from burns and radiation poisoning. But the President and most Americans felt that the bomb's use was justified because it brought an end to World War II.

Imagine that you are a student living at the end of World War II in 1945. Write a letter to the editor of a newspaper voicing your opinion about America's use of the atomic bomb against Japan. Give reasons why you either support the action or why you think it was wrong.

Dear Editor:

Sincerely,

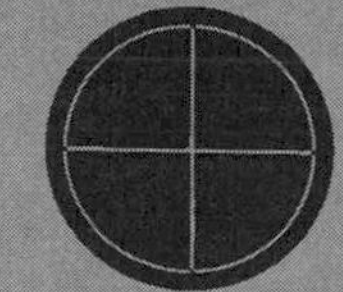

Name ______________________________ Date ____________________

Decide Which Word Does Not Belong

At right are groupings of names and words that appeared in Chapter 5. Underline the one item in each group that does not belong. Then, on the line below, explain how the underlined item is different from the others.

1.	cartridge	gun	bullet
2.	revolver	pistol	rifle
3.	Albert Einstein	Franklin Roosevelt	Harry Truman
4.	Richard Gatling	Hiram Maxim	Ezra Lee
5.	submarine	battleship	destroyer
6.	Robert Oppenheimer	Samuel Colt	Enrico Fermi
7.	Hartford	Hiroshima	Nagasaki
8.	David Bushnell	Richard Gatling	John Holland
9.	Great Britain	Japan	Nevada

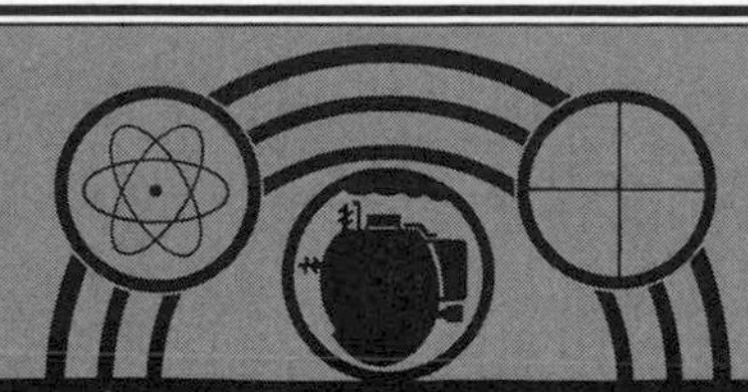

Name ______________________ Date ______________

Solve Some Submarine Math

Create a Graph

On a separate sheet of paper, make a simple bar graph of your own using the information about submarines listed below. Shade or color the bars to differentiate between surface and underwater speeds.

	Surface Speed	Underwater Speed
John Holland's submarine	7 knots	6 knots
World War II-type submarine	21 knots	11 knots
Nuclear submarine	25 knots	30 knots

Change Knots to Miles or Kilometers Per Hour

Look up the word *knot* in a dictionary or encyclopedia. Write down how many miles (kilometers) per hour one knot is equal to. Then compute how fast in mph (kph) John Holland's submarine could travel both on the surface and under the water.

A Bonus Thinking Problem

Why do you think a nuclear-powered submarine can travel faster underwater than on the surface? Write your answer below.

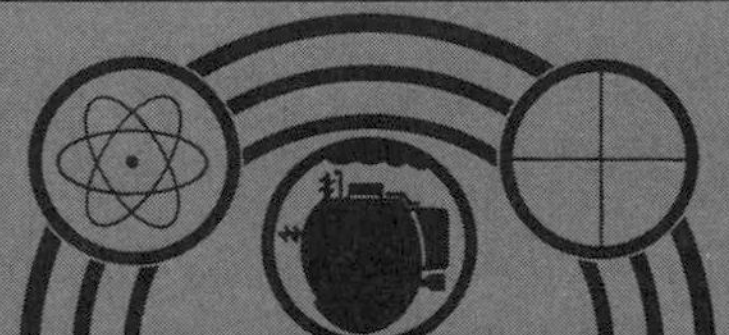

CHAPTER 6

Inventions Help Business and Industry Grow

From the mid-1800s on, numerous inventions gave a boost to business and industry. Several of these inventions were discussed in Chapter 3. This chapter investigates some others.

The Elevator

One of the earliest inventions that benefited business and industry was the elevator. It was developed in 1857 by Elisha Otis of Yonkers, New York.

People have been interested in lifting devices since ancient times. Historians believe the Egyptians used a hand-cranked lift in building the pyramids. The lift probably worked off a system of pulleys and winches. Records show that the ancient Greeks also used such a machine.

Elisha Otis demonstrates his elevator in New York's Crystal Palace in 1853. It was powered by a hydraulic engine.

Elisha Otis's elevator was powered by a hydraulic engine. Hydraulic engines utilize, or use, fluid under pressure. The hydraulic elevator had no cables. It was raised and lowered by the pressure of water in a cylinder. By increasing the pressure on a plunger inside the cylinder, the elevator rose. Releasing the pressure caused the elevator to move down.

The hydraulic elevator could not be installed in tall buildings. The plunger required a pit as deep as the height of the building itself. So when Otis first demonstrated his elevator, it was in a building only five stories high.

Otis's elevator had a safety device to reassure hesitant riders. He demonstrated its reliability himself. Otis rode the elevator to the top floor of the five-story building and ordered its rope cut. To the surprise of all who watched, the elevator did not fall. Instead, two sets of bars automatically attached themselves to the side of the shaft, preventing Otis and his invention from plunging five floors to certain destruction.

Electricity gradually replaced hydraulic power in elevators. The first electric elevator was invented by a German engineer named Werner von Siemens. The first electric elevator to be used in a building was installed by the Otis Brothers Company in New York City in 1889. The "Otis Brothers" were the sons of Elisha Otis.

The Escalator

The escalator made traveling between floors in buildings easier. In this picture from an early drawing, you can see the giant chains and sprockets that drove the moving stairway.

The escalator was another device that helped people move about buildings. It was invented by Jesse Reno, an American, in 1891.

An escalator is a moving stairway. It works like two giant bicycle chains. Two heavy roller chains are moved along by a sprocket powered by an electric motor. Attached to the chains are a series of steps. The steps rise when the escalator is going up and down. They flatten out at each end to allow riders to safely step on and off.

The first escalator was demonstrated at the Paris Exposition in 1900. It was one of many new inventions shown at the exposition, a kind of world fair. One year later, the escalator was brought back to America. The Otis Elevator Company re-installed it in Gimbel Brothers' department store in Philadelphia.

An escalator's passenger capacity is tremendous. As many as five thousand riders can be transported on one in an hour. Traveling at a speed of 90 to 120 feet (27.4–36.6 meters) per minute, the steps quickly can take people to their floor, or level.

Escalators are used in many places today. They are especially popular in department stores, office buildings, and airport terminals.

The Assembly Line

Until the end of the eighteenth century, all goods produced in America were handmade. Skilled craftsmen spent many hours making just one product. Although the quality of goods was excellent, prices were very high. This was because of the time required to produce each item.

Chapter 2 briefly discussed how Henry Ford's assembly line changed the way automobiles were put together. All automobile parts were interchangeable, that is, they fit any car in production. Each worker had only one task to complete. The workers stood at a work station along the assembly line and added a single part to the car.

But the idea of using interchangeable parts began many years earlier with Eli Whitney, the inventor of the cotton gin. Whitney opened a musket factory near New Haven, Connecticut, in 1798. He obtained a contract from the U.S. government to produce ten thousand guns for the army.

Whitney's factory did not make each musket separately. Instead, his plant made machine tools that made individual parts that were then assembled into guns. Before his factory opened, every gun in America was made by hand by a gunsmith. By using previously made parts, Whitney could turn out ten thousand guns for every one produced by a skilled craftsman. The result was a larger quantity of guns at a much cheaper price.

Workers assemble parts for a Model T at the Ford Motor Company.

In 1904, automobile manufacturer Random E. Olds adopted Whitney's methods. By using parts that were interchangeable, he produced five thousand Oldsmobiles in one year. Like Whitney, however, his product was not made on an assembly line. Workers brought each part to a certain place and added it to the car.

It was left to Henry Ford to introduce the assembly line to manufacturing. He installed a moving assembly line at his Michigan plant in 1913. Cars moved slowly along a conveyor belt the length of three football fields. Each worker along the way added one part to the car. An entire vehicle was put together in a minute and a half. Later, the time was reduced to a minute. By 1925, Ford was producing a new car every ten seconds!

Ford's assembly line made mass production possible. Mass production is the making of goods in large quantities. Producing in large quantities decreases the cost of making each item. This is a benefit to the company because it can produce more in a shorter time with more competitive prices. And it's a benefit for the customer who gets to pay lower prices. Almost every product in America today is mass-produced. Not only are goods cheaper, but broken or defective parts can be replaced without the consumer having to buy a new product. Mass production has also led to a division of labor. Workers on an assembly line need only be skilled in a single operation.

The Computer

Two workers are dwarfed by the size of the first all electronic computer, which appeared in 1947. Computers remained large until the invention of the transistor.

No invention revolutionized business and industry more than the computer. In a relatively short time, it replaced the typewriter and lessened the need for file cabinets in most offices.

The computer was invented in 1944 by Howard Aiken. At first it was a large and bulky machine. All early computers, in fact, were huge, and they required a lot of floor space. A computer built by the U.S. Army in 1946 weighed 30 tons and took up 1,500 square feet. That is more space than some smaller houses contain.

Computers remained large until the transistor was invented. The transistor was a small electronic device that replaced vacuum tubes in computers and televisions. It was developed in 1948 by John Bardeen, Walter Brattain, and William Shockley. The transistor made computers smaller, faster, and more affordable.

Between 1948 and 1978, great advancements were made in computers. Integrated circuits appeared in 1958, making it possible to group many transistors in a small space. Next came the silicon chip. The silicon chip led to the development of the PC, or personal computer.

An amazing device, the silicon chip measures only 5 mm square and can pass through the eye of a large needle. It is no larger than a fingernail. Yet, it can handle more information in a second than a person can in many days of work.

Today, computers are used everywhere. They are found in schools, offices, and plants—anywhere people work and play. They are used in airplanes, automobiles, passenger trains, and space shuttles. A large percentage of homes now have personal computers.

In recent years, laptop or notebook computers have become popular. Students and business people find them both convenient and timesaving.

Name ______________________ Date ______________________

Solve These Math Problems

1. By 1925, the Ford Motor Company was producing a car every 10 seconds. How many cars could be made in:

   a. one minute? __________

   b. one hour? __________

   c. an eight-hour workday? __________

   Use the space to work out the answers.

2. The first escalator was demonstrated in Paris in 1900. Paris is 3,636 air miles (5,850 air kilometers) from New York City. How many hours would it take a jet airliner to travel the distance between the two cities at the speeds listed below (round to the nearest hour)?

   a. 400 mph (644 kph) __________

   b. 500 mph (804 kph) __________

   c. 600 mph (965 kph) __________

   Use the space provided to find the answers.

3. A magazine advertised a complete computer system at a 15 percent discount. How much would you pay for the entire system if the computer, along with a printer, normally costs

Name ______________________ *Date* ______________________

Test Your Critical Thinking Skills

Computers have had a tremendous impact on the lives of all people. Use your ability to think critically and respond to the questions on this page about these modern devices. Continue on a separate piece of paper if necessary.

1. Have computers caused workers to lose jobs, or has the computer industry created more opportunities for employment? What does the future hold for people, computers, and jobs?

____

____

____

____

2. How are computers beneficial in schools and classrooms? List as many ways as you can.

____

____

____

____

____

3. *BONUS QUESTION.* Your family may not own a personal computer, but chances are there are several other kinds of computers in your home. Can you think of two?

____

____

____

____

____

____

Name ______________________ *Date* ______________

Improve Your Map Skills

Look in an atlas or another source containing maps and fill in the blanks in the paragraphs below.

1. Eli Whitney opened a musket factory in New Haven, Connecticut. The capital of Connecticut is ______________. To reach the capital, Mr. Whitney had to travel (in which direction?) ______________________.

   Due west of Connecticut is the state of __________. Its capital is __________. Due east is the state of __________, whose capital is ______________.

2. The first elevator was installed in a building in New York City. New York City is located in the ______________ part of New York State. To reach ______________, the capital of the state, one would have to travel (in which direction?) ______________ from New York City.

   By driving northwest from the capital, one would reach the ______________ Mountains. By driving due east, one would enter the state of __________. This state's capital is __________.

3. Henry Ford built his automobile plant at Highland Park, Michigan. Highland Park is a suburb of the larger city of __________.

   To reach the state capital of Michigan, Mr. Ford had to drive (in which direction?) ______________. Michigan's capital is ______________________.

   In addition to parts of Canada, Michigan is bordered by three states. They are ______________, ______________, and ______________________.

4. The escalator was introduced at the Paris Exposition in France. France is a country on the continent of ______________. France's neighbor to the southwest is __________. Several countries border France on the east. Two of these are ______________ and ______________.

   The city of Paris is located on the ______________ River. This important river flows northwest and empties into the __________ Channel. Directly across this channel is the island of __________.

Name ______________________________ Date ____________________

Complete a Word Search

Below are twenty-one words from Chapter 6. Find and circle each in the word search. They may run horizontally, vertically, or diagonally. None are inverted, or backwards.

ASSEMBLY
ELEVATOR
MANUFACTURE
CABLE
ESCALATOR
MASS
CHIP
EXPOSITION
MUSKET
CIRCUIT
GUNSMITH
SILICON
COMPUTER
HYDRAULIC
SPROCKET
CONSUMER
INTERCHANGEABLE
TRANSISTOR
CYLINDER
MACHINE
VACUUM

C O N S U M E R G W K C I C R Z Y S X
O P T K G E X S I R V C F O X P T S J
M U S K E T P P E W M B T P A C L X L
P L O U M M O R C Y B A E U R W Z Q B
U R H P I A S O L D V A C U U M N N G
T Y W W M N I C M E Y F M L F F K D O
E P J T T U T K L M W D N M Y B U I S
R L X I R F I E S C A L A T O R S T H
O M Z H F A O T R X Y C I R C U I T F
Y Z Z R W C N H I C P L H U M I W T N
F W M Z D T H S Z C H T I I V Q X C Q
Z G M K G U Z I I R M A H N N T J B S
W U W D H R A L P S R O N O D E B K C
X N D P C E U I T S T E S G G E Q S I
A S D P Q A M C A B W O Z Y E W R O V
N M H X R I O O A Z M A R P Y A W Y H
N I E D D W M N W B Z A S S E M B L Y
I T Y O B Q K N V E L B S U F Q C L R
Q H J J M A M A H K R E K S Y F O B E

CHAPTER 7

Timesaving Appliances Improve Home Life

One might find it difficult to visualize a home today without a refrigerator or washing machine. Or a sewing machine, a vacuum cleaner, or an electric iron, for that matter. Yet, until the middle of the nineteenth century, none of these conveniences existed.

Beginning in 1845, appliances began to appear that did much to ease the drudgery of household work. The result was an improvement in the quality of life for most Americans and an increased amount of time for leisure activities.

Elias Howe's sewing machine, which he patented in 1846. Howe's machine was the first practical one on the market.

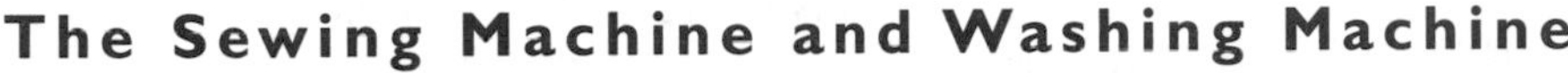

The Sewing Machine and Washing Machine

The first two appliances to be used in the home had to do with the making and cleaning of clothes. Elias Howe patented the sewing machine in 1846, and Hamilton E. Smith patented the washing machine in 1858.

Actually, it was Walter Hunt, the inventor of the safety pin, who built the first sewing machine. But Hunt never applied for a patent. Credit therefore went to Elias Howe of Boston, Massachusetts.

Howe's machine was simple. A wheel turned by hand caused a needle to go up and down through cloth. Although an improvement over stitching by hand, Howe's invention had a major drawback. Cloth being sewn was pinned to a metal strip that moved with each stitch. Since the metal strip—with the pins protruding from it was only a few inches long, it was necessary to move and re-pin the cloth many times in order to complete a seam.

The flaws in Howe's sewing machine were corrected by another inventor. In 1851, Isaac M. Singer replaced the hand-turned wheel with a foot pedal, making the machine easier to use. Singer also eliminated the short metal plate to which the cloth was pinned. With his machine, the material rested on a flat table and passed under a needle that sewed in a straight line. Later, electric motors replaced the foot pedal in Singer's sewing machines.

The first washing machine was hand cranked, cumbersome, and hard-to-use.

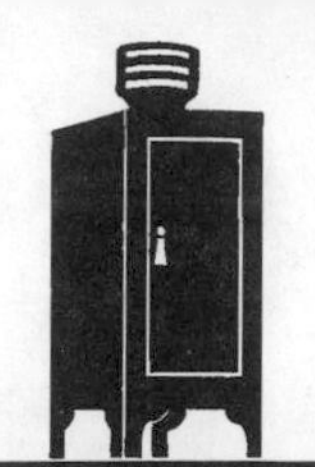

The first washing machine offered some relief from the hard work of washing clothes. But like the early sewing machine, it had certain drawbacks. It consisted of a number of revolving paddles in a wooden tub. The operator of the machine turned a hand crank that turned the paddles. Not only was Hamilton Smith's washer tiring to use, but the paddles sometimes damaged the clothes.

One of the first vacuum cleaners, which appeared on the market around the turn of the 20th century.

In 1910, the electric washer replaced Smith's crude device. This washer was invented by Alva J. Fisher. It featured an agitator that swished the clothes around until they were clean. Unlike modern machines, Fisher's washer could not rinse and spin the load. Clothes were run through a wringer that was operated by a hand crank. Wringers remained a part of washing machines until after World War II.

The Carpet Sweeper and the Vacuum Cleaner

Dirt in rugs and carpets was a problem for housekeepers for centuries. The only way to remove these dirt particles was to hang a rug on a line and beat it vigorously with a rug beater.

Then, in 1876, Melville Bissell invented the carpet sweeper. The carpet sweeper was a simple device that had a revolving brush inside a dust pan. As the operator pushed the sweeper back and forth by its handle, the brush picked up the dirt and deposited it in the pan. Carpet sweepers soon gave way to vacuum cleaners, but the sweeper never fell completely out of use. Many households continue to use them today for small cleanup tasks.

There is disagreement as to who invented the vacuum cleaner. Some historians give the credit to John S. Thurman in 1899. Others say that H. C. Booth invented the machine in 1901. Regardless, the vacuum cleaner made housekeeping quicker and easier. It also eliminated the dust that swirled through rooms when they were swept with a broom. And, like other appliances, it made more time available for other activities.

The vacuum cleaner removes dirt from carpets by creating a vacuum. A vacuum is a space almost completely empty of air. The vacuum is created by an

air pump driven by an electric motor. This causes a suction that draws the dirt into a bag in the cleaner. Today's machines have disposable bags that are discarded when they become full.

The Electric Light Bulb

An entire chapter of this book could be devoted to the inventor of the electric light bulb: Thomas Alva Edison, one of the greatest inventors of all time. He patented almost 1,100 inventions and worked on many more. Three for which he is well-known are the light bulb, the phonograph, and the talking motion picture. This section deals with the light bulb.

Like most inventors, Edison's interest in discovery began early. As a boy, he sold newspapers on a train. The train made a daily trip to and from his hometown. The conductor gave young Thomas permission to set up a small laboratory in the baggage car. There, Edison happily printed his own short newspaper and sold it to the passengers. In this laboratory, he also carried out experiments. He mixed different things together to see what he could come up with. It wasn't long before Edison set the baggage car on fire, and the conductor threw him off the train.

When he grew up, Edison built a laboratory at Menlo Park, New Jersey. He began working on the light bulb in 1878. Several scientists before him had developed lighting, but their inventions were not practical. The filament, or the part inside the bulb that produced the light, burned out quickly. There were also no switches, sockets, or way to make electricity to light the bulbs.

Edison, along with his assistants, sometimes worked day and night trying to perfect a light bulb. They often ate their meals at their work desks. But they were determined to make the light bulb practical. Finally, in October 1879, they made a filament of carbonized, or scorched, sewing thread. It was successful. The light bulb they produced burned for forty hours. Later, a strong metal called tungsten replaced thread as the filament in light bulbs. The modern light bulb was born.

Three years after developing his light bulb, Edison opened the Pearl Street Power Station in New York City. Money for the station came from a group of wealthy businessmen. By 1885, the plant was supplying electricity for 250,000 lights in New York City. Edison's station joined with another, and the two later became the famous General Electric Company.

The electric bulb brought improvements to both home life and the business world. Lighting made it easier for people to accomplish things at

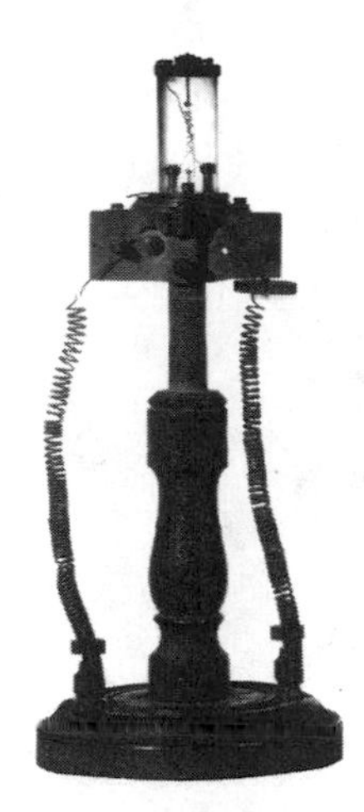

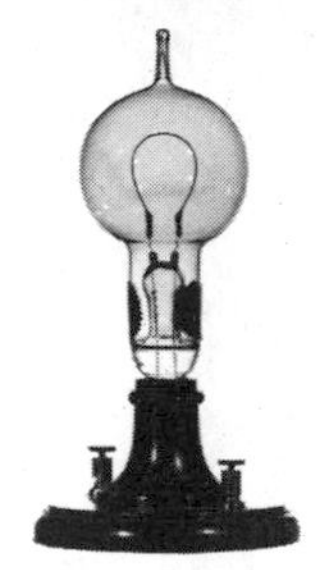

Illustrates the development of the lightbulb. The top bulb is Thomas Edison's first light bulb, which he patented in 1879.

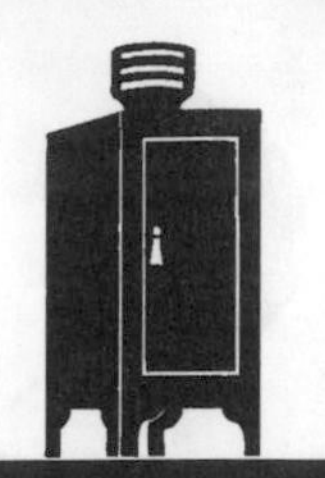

home after dark. Stores could stay open longer hours, and lights could advertise what the stores sold. Electric street lights made the streets safer. Everyone's life was touched by Edison's wonderful accomplishment.

Refrigeration

An early refrigerator, which gradually replaced the icebox in most American homes. The refrigerant Freon® made the electric refrigerator possible.

Refrigeration, or the process of cooling, is a relatively recent development. Electric refrigerators and air conditioners did not come into general use until the 1930s.

For many years, the insulated icebox was standard equipment in most homes. A huge block of ice in the box preserved food for a short time. The icebox, however, had several drawbacks. A block of ice did not last long, especially in the hot summer months. And when the block melted, the homeowner had quite a mess to clean up.

The electric refrigerator was a big improvement over the icebox. Food could be kept much longer without spoiling, and a freezer compartment allowed meats and vegetables to be frozen and preserved indefinitely.

Although the refrigerator was not an American invention, an American chemist is given credit for the refrigerant that cooled it. In 1930, Thomas Midgley developed the gas Freon®. At the time, and for some sixty years afterwards, Freon® was considered safe to use. Now scientists know that it poses a threat to the ozone layer that protects the Earth from harmful ultraviolet rays. Freon's® use is being discontinued, and a search goes on for a safer replacement.

An American did invent air conditioning. Willis S. Carrier received a patent for it in 1902. He later formed the Carrier Corporation that is today a major manufacturer of air conditioners.

Air conditioning at first consisted of window units that cooled one or more rooms. Central air conditioning to cool entire houses and buildings did not appear until much later. Today, many homes have heat pumps that cool in the summer and provide heat in the winter.

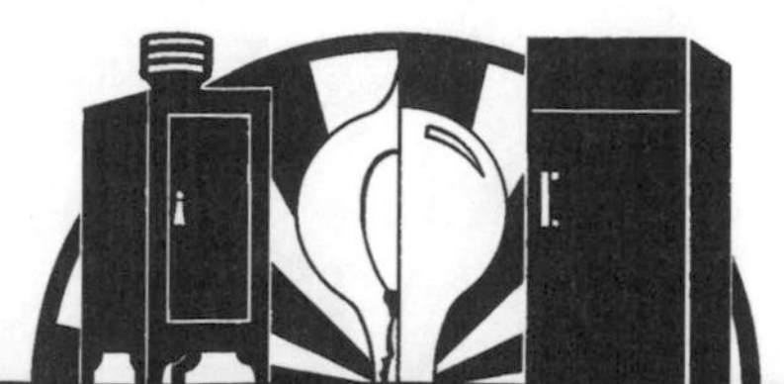

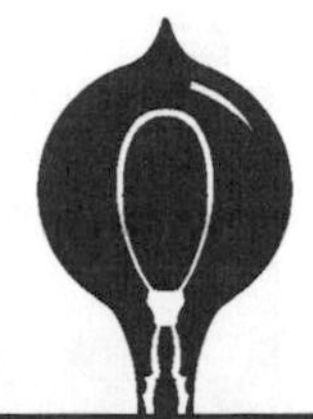

Like refrigerators, air conditioners use Freon®. The Freon® flows through a series of tubes, where cold air and hot air change it from a liquid to a gas. In this state, it absorbs the heat from inside the unit and brings about refrigeration.

Refrigeration has made life better for everyone. Because of the refrigerator, people can eat foods that are both nutritious and safe. And air conditioning makes the hot, humid months of summer more bearable.

The Microwave Oven

No convenience has become more popular in modern times than the microwave oven—an electronic stove that cooks food with short radio waves. These waves are produced by an electronic vacuum tube called a magnetron. The microwaves travel from the magnetron to the stirrer, which is similar to a small fan. The stirrer causes the waves to bounce from wall to wall. In doing so, they enter the food and cook it from the inside out.

A woman demonstrates cooking a hamburger in the Raytheon Radarange, and early microwave oven. Microwave ovens became commercially available in 1952.

The idea for the microwave oven came about by accident. One day in 1946, Dr. Percy Spencer of the Raytheon Company was working near a magnetron. The magnetron apparently had a leak somewhere. When Dr. Spencer removed a candy bar from his pocket, he noticed that it had melted. Did the magnetron have anything to do with the candy melting? He wondered.

The following day, Dr. Spencer brought a bag of popcorn kernels to the laboratory. He spread some kernels near the magnetron. In a short time, the kernels were popping all over the place. Dr. Spencer realized that microwaves could be used to cook food.

Raytheon began working on a microwave oven immediately. But it was the Tappan Company that produced the first unit that was sold commercially. The year was 1952, and the oven sold for $1,295! Today one can purchase a microwave oven for as little as $100.

Name ______________________________ Date ____________________

Think It Through

Barthelemy Thimonnier, a French tailor, invented an early sewing machine in 1830. His invention did not stay on the market long, however. An angry mob attacked his factory in Paris and wrecked his machines.

At about the same time, the American inventor Walter Hunt also came out with a workable sewing machine. But he never patented it.

Why do you suppose a mob destroyed Thimonnier's machines? Which group of workers do you think made up the mob? And why do you think Hunt never applied for a patent?

Write your thoughts on the lines at left.

On a separate piece of paper, choose an invention discussed in this chapter that you think was the most important. Tell why. Which was the most help to the American housekeeper, and why?

Name ______________________________ Date ____________________

Solve These Math Problems

1. A beef pot pie must cook in a microwave oven for $5\,^1/_2$ minutes. If only one pie can be cooked at a time, how long would it take to prepare 6 pies?

   ________________ minutes

2. Isaac Singer was a pioneer of the installment plan. The installment plan allows a consumer to make a purchase and pay for it in equal monthly installments, or payments.

   Imagine that you buy an appliance that costs $582.40. Also, imagine that there is no interest or carrying charge. You make a down payment of $100.00 and agree to pay the balance in 12 installments.

   How much will you have to pay each month?

   $_____________

3. You have three baskets of clothes to wash and dry. It takes about 35 minutes for your washing machine to go through the complete wash cycle. It takes another hour for your dryer to dry a load.

   How much total time is needed to wash and dry the three loads separately?

   _______ hours and ______ minutes

4. The average life of a 60-watt light bulb is 1,000 hours. A light left on for 1,000 continuous hours would burn for __________ days.

Name ______________________________ *Date* ____________________

Research an Invention

Not every invention that aided homeowners was discussed in Chapter 7. Many others appeared in the years between the latter part of the nineteenth century and the present. Three of these were the electric iron, the toaster, and the dishwasher. You can probably think of many more.

Research any home-related invention not covered in this chapter. Answer the questions about it at right.

1. What is the invention you researched? ______________________
2. Who invented it? ______________________
3. What year was it invented? ______________________
4. How did it benefit people? ______________________

____

____

5. Briefly describe how the invention worked.

____

____

____

____

____

____

6. In the space below, or on another piece of paper, draw a picture of the invention.

Name ______________________ Date ______________________

Test Your Vocabulary in Context

Fill in the blanks in the sentences using the words below.

- advanced
- cool
- next
- bring
- dreamed
- progress
- clothes
- enjoy
- switch
- comfortable
- future
- technology
- conveniences
- hot
- touched
- vacuum

Inventions have ______________________ the lives of all of us. Because of ______________________ in science and ______________________, we ______________________ things our ancestors never ______________________ of.

We go to the refrigerator when we want a ______________ drink. We turn on the air conditioner when we are ______________. We ______________ the carpets or rugs to keep them clean. We ______________ on the lights when the house is dark. When our ______________ are dirty, we put them in the washer. We certainly lead more ______________ lives than people did years ago.

The many ______________ we enjoy today have been around only about 150 years. What will the ______________ 150 years ______________? Do you think people in the ______________ will look back on us as being not very ______________?

CHAPTER 8

Greater Opportunities for Entertainment Appear

By the end of the nineteenth century, Americans had more leisure time than ever before. And new inventions began to appear that helped satisfy their need for recreation and amusement.

A group of ladies (and one gentleman) don earphones and listen to an early phonograph. Note the rapt attention on the faces of all the listeners.

Two of these inventions were the work of Thomas Edison. In 1877 he invented the phonograph, or record player. Eleven years later he produced a motion picture camera with which he made the first short movies. It is easy to see why this famous inventor was called the "Wizard of Menlo Park."

The Phonograph

The phonograph was Thomas Edison's favorite invention. No inventor before him had attempted to make anything resembling it. And it worked the first time he tried it! It also made him famous.

Edison's phonograph did not use a record. Sound was recorded on a cylinder covered with tin foil. Edison later replaced the tin foil with hard wax. Gradually, a rubber disk took the place of the cylinder, and the record was born. In time, plastic instead of rubber was used to make records.

In a phonograph, the vibrations of a needle are carried to a loudspeaker. The loudspeaker sends out sound waves. A record itself is made with grooves that contain tiny differences. As the record revolves on a turntable, the needle moves along these grooves. Each irregularity or difference in the grooves produces a different sound that is heard by the listener.

The First Simple Movies

Thomas Edison did not invent the motion picture. But he invented two machines that produced the first pictures to move on a screen.

In 1888, Edison developed the kinetograph. This was a camera that made a series of photographs. A few years later, he invented the kinetoscope. The kinetoscope was a device for showing the pictures made with the camera. The kinetoscope was nothing more than a large box with a peephole and a crank. For a penny, the viewer could look through the peephole, turn the crank, and watch the pictures move.

Thomas Edison's kinetoscope, which provided viewers with their first glimpse of moving pictures. One squinted through a peephole, turned a crank, and beheld action scenes in motion (such as that at right).

The first of these simple movies was entitled *Fred Ott's Sneeze.* And that is all it was: a short film of a man sneezing. Edison also made pictures of men boxing and people dancing. Crude as these first films were, they marked the beginning of the motion picture industry.

About the year 1914, Edison made the first talking movie. This he accomplished by using his phonograph and movie camera at the same time. But there were so many flaws in this method that it never caught on. The first real motion picture with sound was *The Jazz Singer,* which was produced in 1927 by Warner Brothers.

Television

Young people today may think that television has been around for a long time. But television is a relatively new form of entertainment. It did not become popular until the 1950s.

The first television sets were somewhat impractical. They were large and bulky and had a picture screen of only about five inches. Picture quality was poor, and the choice of programs was very limited.

Television was invented in the early 1920s. Credit for its development is given to a Russian-born American physicist named Vladimir Zworykin.

A family enjoys a program on an early console-style television. This picture is most likely from the early 1950s, when television found its way into the American home.

Zworykin came to America from Russia in 1919. In 1920, he went to work for the Westinghouse Electric Company. There he began experimenting with ways to transmit live pictures through the air. In 1923, he patented the first television camera, which he called an iconoscope. One year later, he received a patent for the kinescope, or television picture tube. With these inventions, he was able to show that sending pictures through the air was possible.

World War II interrupted the production of television. All of America's resources were directed toward the war effort. Once the war was successfully concluded, television production began again. But it took another decade for this new form of entertainment to catch on with the American public. Early television sets were expensive, and few Americans could afford them. Also, many people saw television as nothing more than a novelty. They seemed content just to stand on sidewalks and watch televised events through the windows of department stores.

Gradually, the price of television sets decreased, and more people bought them. The quality of programs also improved. Many shows that had been successful on radio switched over to television in the late 1950s. Color television was introduced and the popularity of television grew even more. By the end of the 1970s, more than 90 percent of American households had at least one television set.

Other Home Entertainment Inventions

Many developments in home entertainment were contributed by other nations. These include the tape recorder and the compact disc. However, Americans have made strides in this area. American inventions include the long-playing record and the VCR (video cassette recorder).

The tape recorder was invented in 1898 by a twenty-year-old Danish engineer named Valdemar Poulsen. Although it did not come into use until about 1935, the tape recorder was first demonstrated at the Paris Exposition of 1900. (You may recall that the escalator was introduced to the world at this same exposition.)

Walter S. Gifford, president of A.T.&T. saw and spoke with President Herbert Hoover during the first public demonstration of television in 1927.

America did contribute the long-playing record, which the compact disc supplanted. Inventor Peter Goldmark invented the 33⅓ rpm record in 1947. It replaced the 78 rpm. *Rpm* stands for "revolutions per minute." The more revolutions, or turns, a record makes, the faster it plays. By reducing the revolutions to 33⅓ a minute, a record turns more slowly. Thus, Goldmark gave the world a record that provided 20 minutes of music instead of the 4½ minutes of the 78 rpm.

Sony of Japan and the Philips Company of the Netherlands developed the compact disc in 1979. The disc gradually replaced the long-playing record. A disc measures 12 centimeters (about 4.7 inches) in diameter. One side provides up to an hour of music or sound. Compared to a record, a compact disc has near-perfect sound quality.

Although the first VCR designed for home use was another Philips contribution, credit for the first video recording goes to an American company. Mincom, a branch of the 3M Scotch Company, first demonstrated black-and-white video recording in 1951. Three years later, the American company built the first professional recorder.

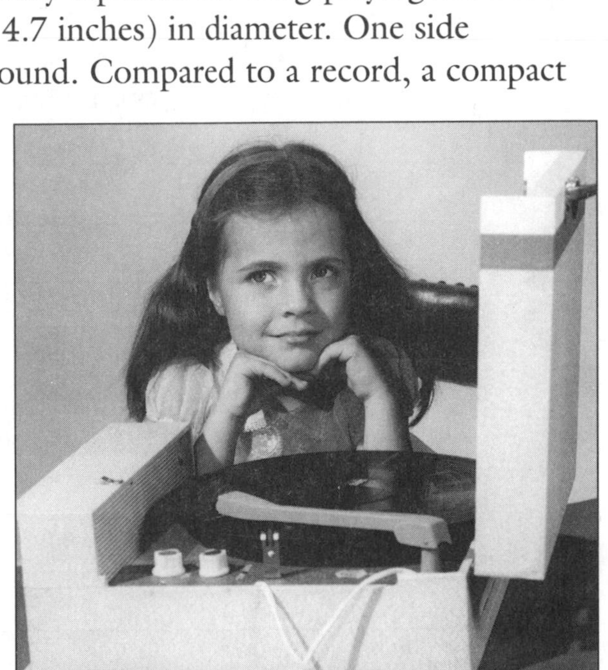

A young girl dreamily listens to a 78 rpm record she is playing on her phonograph. 78 rpm records were popular until 1947, when the 33⅓ record was developed.

Name ______________________________ Date ____________________

Is TV Beneficial?

No invention has influenced people more than television. In the 1950s, TV replaced radio as the most popular form of home entertainment. It also challenged movie theaters as the favorite form of recreation in America.

Television has both supporters and critics. Like most developments with such an impact, it has both advantages and disadvantages. With this in mind, respond to the questions at right.

1. What are four ways in which television is beneficial?

____

____

____

____

2. What are three criticisms or negative things about television?

____

____

____

____

3. How many hours of television are you permitted to watch on school nights? on weekends? If your parent(s) or guardian(s) does not place limits on your television viewing, explain why.

____

____

____

4. Does your parent(s) or guardian(s) monitor the programs you watch on television? Why or why not?

____

____

____

____

Name ______________________________ Date ____________________

Improve Your Geography Skills

Vladimir Zworykin, the inventor of television, was born and raised in Russia. Before he immigrated to the United States in 1919, he received a degree in electrical engineering from the Petrograd Institute of Technology.

With the city of Petrograd, Russia, in mind, look up Russia or the Union of Socialist Soviet Republics in an encyclopedia and answer the questions.

1. The city of Petrograd did not receive that name until 1914, when World War I broke out. For many years it was called after the name of the czar who founded it in 1713. From 1713 to 1914, the city was called ______________________.
2. The name of the above city was changed again in 1924 when the Communists seized control of Russia. They changed the name to ______________________.
3. After the Soviet Union collapsed in 1991, the city was once again called ______________________.
4. Find what was once called Petrograd on a map of Russia. It is located on a well-known gulf called the Gulf of ______________.
5. To the north of the city is the largest lake in Europe. This lake is Lake ______________________.
6. The city that was once called Petrograd lies at about 60 degrees north latitude. One degree of latitude represents 69 miles (111 kilometers). Each degree tells how many miles a certain area on a map is from the equator, which is 0 degrees latitude.

   Moving east on your map, you will notice that the capitals of Finland, Sweden, and Norway are at about the same latitude as the city you are researching. Write the capitals of these countries on the blank lines before their names.

   ______________ Finland

   ______________ Sweden

   ______________ Norway

7. Remembering that one degree equals 69 miles (111 kilometers), how far are Petrograd and the capitals above from the equator?

   ________ miles (or kilometers)

Name ______________________ Date ______________

Broaden Your Vocabulary

Have you ever wondered how certain inventions and devices acquired their names?

Names for things are formed in several ways. Sometimes, two words are combined to create a name. *Steamboat* is an example. *Steam* and *boat* are joined to create a new word.

Some names are the result of combining a word with a prefix. A prefix is a word part added to the beginning of a word. *Microwave* is a word formed by adding the prefix *micro* to *wave*. *Micro* means "very small."

Finally, some names for things come from combining a word with a suffix. A suffix is a word part added to the end of a word. An example is *cablegram*. The suffix *gram* means "a message." Thus, a cablegram is a message sent by cable.

Listed below are the words, prefixes, and suffixes that were used to create the names for the inventions discussed in Chapter 8. Look each up in an advanced dictionary and write its meaning.

1. vide (Latin) ______________________

2. tele- ______________________

3. kinetic ______________________

4. -graph ______________________

5. scope ______________________

6. icono- ______________________

7. phono- ______________________

Name ______________________ *Date* ______________

Conduct An Interview About Radio

Although television replaced the radio as an important means of home entertainment, the radio by no means disappeared from American homes. Almost 93 million households still had radios in the 1990s.

The radio was not an American contribution. It was invented in 1895 by an Italian electrical engineer, Guglielmo Marconi. But it quickly became popular in America. The first radio station appeared in 1920. Ten years later there were 600 across the country. By 1950 there were 2,000, and this number increased to 4,000 by 1970. In 1990, there were about 9,000 stations on the air in the United States.

Interview several older people who grew up when radio was supreme in the American home. Ask them to compare radio with television. Ask them which they like better, and why. Also, ask them to comment on their favorite past radio programs.

Record your findings on the lines below.

CHAPTER 9

Other Discoveries Aid the Consumer

You have seen how electricity and home appliances made life easier for the American consumer. In Chapter 9, you will learn about other products that improved the quality of American life even more.

Plastics make in-line skating safe for this young boy. Not only are his skates made of plastic, but so are his helmet and pads. Plastic helps protect him from serious injury should he fall.

Plastics

The story of the invention of plastics is interesting. Would you believe it had something to do with a pool, or billiard, ball?

Until the middle of the nineteenth century, many products were made of ivory. Among these were billiard balls, piano keys, and knife handles. But ivory was expensive and hard to get. Its use also angered people who strongly object to killing helpless animals to obtain it. For these reasons, manufacturers began searching for a substitute to use in its place.

A suitable replacement for ivory was found shortly after the Civil War. Phelan and Collender, a New York company that made billiard balls, staged a contest in 1868. They offered a prize of $10,000 to anyone who could develop a substitute for ivory.

Inventors nationwide set to work. John Wesley Hyatt, a New Jersey inventor, was one of these. Assisted by his brother Isaiah, he began experimenting with carbon compounds. One of these was pyroxylin. Another was camphor. Pyroxylin is formed from cellulose, which is the woody part of plants and trees, and nitric acid. Camphor is a substance with a strong odor that is used—among other things—to make moth balls. By combining pyroxylin and camphor under heat and pressure, John Hyatt produced celluloid, the first plastic.

Hyatt won the $10,000 prize, and Phelan and Collender began turning out plastic billiard balls. Hyatt afterwards found other uses for his invention. Soon, piano keys, combs, dental plates, toys, and other items were being made of plastic.

Today, there are about sixty different kinds of plastics used in every imaginable product. Some of these—such as cellophane and nylon—will be discussed later in this chapter.

Frozen Foods

Frozen dinners have made meal preparation easier and faster resulting in people spending less time in the kitchen and more time enjoying leisure activities.

Clarence Birdseye was an American inventor and industrialist. In 1912, he accompanied a fur-trading expedition to Labrador, part of the Canadian province of Newfoundland. While there, he noticed that fish caught by the inhabitants froze stiff as soon as they were taken from the water. And he found out that these same fish—when thawed, cooked, and eaten—were just as flavorable as those that were fresh.

Birdseye's observations gave him an idea. If fish could be frozen and preserved, why not other foods? Why couldn't vegetables, fruits, and other meats be treated in the same way?

From 1917 to 1924, Birdseye experimented with freezing foods. His goal was to reproduce the fast-dry freezing that occurs in Arctic regions. He worked hard on this for seven years. In 1924, he came up with a method of quick-freezing foods between two refrigerated metal plates. He also thought of the idea of freezing foods in small, packageable blocks.

Birdseye's method of fast freezing proved successful in preserving a variety of foodstuffs. With a group of friends, he formed Birdseye General Foods in 1924. He began by selling frozen fish and vegetables. Later, he started packaging other frozen foods.

After a few years, Birdseye sold his company to a firm that later became the General Foods Corporation. General Foods agreed that the Birdseye name, split into two words, would be used on its brands. That is how Birds Eye products came into being. The deal with General Foods earned Clarence Birdseye $22 million.

From fresh meats and vegetables, the frozen food industry expanded to precooked meals. One of the first precooked meals was chicken fricassee. It consisted of chicken served in a sauce made with its own gravy. All one had to do was place the frozen meal in the oven for a specified amount of time, and it was ready to eat.

Today, almost any kind of food or meal can be bought frozen. And with the invention of the microwave oven, frozen foods are even more popular than they were in Birdseye's day.

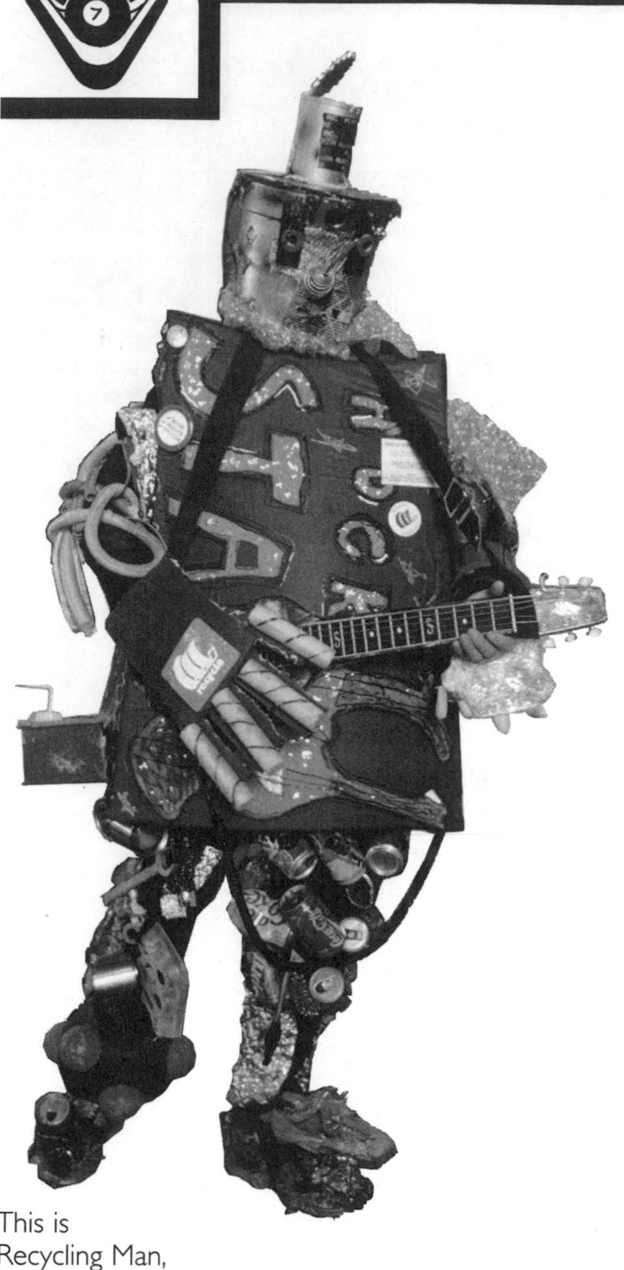

This is Recycling Man, who reminds us that modern conveniences have made for more trash, adding to environmental pollution. Each of us can help by recycling all of the plastic and aluminum we use.

Aluminum Foil

Another product that excited consumers was aluminum foil. Its introduction in 1947 changed the way many foods were cooked and stored.

The development of aluminum foil had nothing to do with food or cooking. It grew out of a need by tobacco and candy companies for a material that would better protect their products from moisture. The tin-lead wrap these companies had used for years was not completely satisfactory.

In 1940, Richard S. Reynolds (nephew of tobacco king R. R. Reynolds) founded the Reynolds Metal Company. Reynolds made aluminum goods. Included among these were aluminum pots, pans, and utensils for American homes. Richard Reynolds also began working to develop a foil with which to line cigarette packages.

Because aluminum is light and soft, it can be molded into many shapes. It can also be pressed into thin sheets. That is what the Reynolds Metal Company managed to do in 1947. The company produced a foil in sheets that were only 7/1000 of an inch (18/1000 of a cm) thick. The foil was not only lightweight, but it was nonrusting and nontoxic as well. It was exactly what the cigarette and candy manufacturers were looking for.

Even though aluminum foil was developed as an aid to industry, it was in the home that it attained its greatest popularity. Consumers found it very handy to have around the house. It was used to cover racks and to line pans in ovens. It was also great for wrapping foods to be stored in the refrigerator. Some people even used aluminum foil to extend the "rabbit ears" on their television sets! Such television buffs claimed that foil improved reception.

Cellophane, Nylon Stockings, Other Plastics

Plastics, frozen foods, and aluminum foil were just three inventions that improved consumers' lives. There were many more.

One was cellophane. Cellophane is a thin, transparent foil used for packaging. It is a kind of plastic. Cellophane was not an American invention. It was developed in 1908 by a Swiss chemist named Jacques Edwin Brandenberger. Brandenberger at the time was trying to come up with a stainproof tablecloth.

Cellophane was introduced in the United States in 1924. First sold by Du Pont Cellophane of Wilmington, Delaware, it quickly became popular as a food wrap.

Nylon is another kind of plastic. It was invented in 1938 by Dr. Wallace H. Carothers of Du Pont. It took thirteen years of research and $27 million to create. Once produced, however, it was used to make many products. Parachutes, fishing line, clothes, toothbrushes, and strings for tennis racquets were some of the things made from nylon.

Nylon stockings, made from plastic, were inexpensive and within the budget of every woman. They replaced costlier silk stockings that had been worn for years.

But one of the most popular uses of nylon was in the production of women's hosiery. Until 1938, women's stockings were made mostly of silk. Silk made for a strong stocking, but it was quite expensive. Nylon provided a way to make a cheaper and more durable stocking.

Nylon stockings were an immediate sensation. When they went on sale on May 15, 1940, long lines formed at department stores throughout America. In some places, near riots broke out as women pushed and shoved to buy the new hosiery. Thirty-six million pairs of nylons were sold between May and December of that year.

Vinyl, Formica, and polyester were three other kinds of plastics that found their way into the home. Vinyl was produced in 1928 and was used in such products as tablecloths and shower curtains. Formica appeared in 1938 and served as a cover for kitchen counter tops. Polyester was developed in 1940 and was used in clothing.

This chapter discussed only a handful of the products that made home life more comfortable for the average American. There were, of course, many others. And new discoveries are being made every day. There seems to be no limit to what science and technology can produce for the consumer.

Name ______________________ *Date* ______________

Make a Chart Based on a Plastic Hunt

If you look around your home, you will see many things that are either plastic or contain plastic. Every room you walk through probably has something in it that is made of plastic. On the chart, list all the plastic items you can find in each of the designated rooms.

Plastic Items in My Home

Kitchen	Bathroom	Bedroom	Den or Living Room
______	______	______	______
______	______	______	______
______	______	______	______
______	______	______	______
______	______	______	______
______	______	______	______
______	______	______	______
______	______	______	______
______	______	______	______
______	______	______	______
______	______	______	______
______	______	______	______
______	______	______	______
______	______	______	______
______	______	______	______

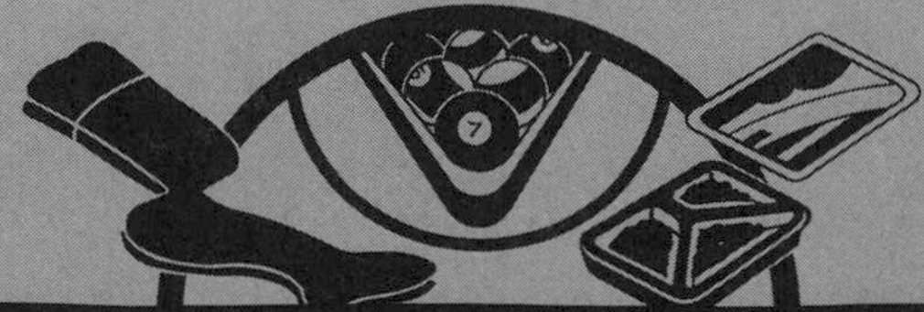

Name ______________________________ *Date* ______________________

Solve a Consumer Products Crossword

Across

2 Once used to make billiard balls.

3 Nylon and cellophane are types of __________.

7 He gave the world frozen food.

9 He invented celluloid.

10 Aluminum _______

11 General _______ Corporation

13 The first frozen food

Down

1 Plastic used in shower curtains

4 Nationality of cellophane's inventor

5 Where Birdseye went in 1912

6 His company developed aluminum foil.

8 ______ stockings

12 Nylon stockings replaced this kind

Name ______________________ Date ______________

Try These Word Problems

Solve using either the U.S. Customary or the metric measurement system.

1. Wrap-It Aluminum Foil comes in three sizes. Their costs are:
   Size A: 25 square feet (2 sq. meter) roll box—$.75
   Size B: 75 square feet (7 sq. meter) roll box—$1.80
   Size C: 200 square feet (19 sq. meter) roll box—$4.06
   On a separate sheet of paper, figure the cost of one square foot or meter of foil in each box. Write your answers on the lines provided.

   Cost of one square foot (meter) of Size A ______________

   Cost of one square foot (meter) of Size B ______________

   Cost of one square foot (meter) of Size C ______________

   Which size box is the best buy? ______________

2. There are 200 square feet (19 sq. meters) of wrap in a large box of Wrap-It Plastic Wrap. The contents of the roll measures 66 2/3 yards (61 meters). If someone laid the entire roll out on the ground, how many feet (or meters) would it cover? Write your answer on the line provided.

   It would cover ______________ feet (meters).

3. The 200 square feet (19 sq. meters) roll of wrap costs $2.07. A 100 square-foot (9.5 sq. meter) roll of the same brand costs $1.35. If you needed 400 square feet (38 sq. meters) of plastic wrap, how much money would you save by buying two 200 square foot-rolls (19 sq. meter) instead of four 100 square-foot rolls (9.5 sq. meter)? Write your answer on the line provided.

   You would save $__________.

Name ______________________________ Date ____________________

Arrange in Chronological Order

Read back over Chapter 9. Then, using numbers 1 through 8, arrange the following events in the order in which they occurred.

________ John Hyatt invents celluloid.

________ Clarence Birdseye goes to Labrador.

________ Aluminum foil is introduced.

________ Clarence Birdseye sells his first frozen foods.

________ The Reynolds Metal Company is founded.

________ Cellophane is invented.

________ Dr. Wallace H. Carothers invents nylon.

________ Vinyl is developed.

Name ______________________ *Date* ______________

Test Your Vocabulary and Spelling Skills

Unscramble the names of six inventions. Write them correctly on the line next to each.

H A P E L C L O N E ______________________

L O N N Y ______________________

O L I F ______________________

S C A L P I T ______________________

L I V N Y ______________________

M O C R A F I ______________________

CHAPTER 10

Technology Makes Space Exploration a Reality

Humans have dreamed of flying in space for hundreds of years. The first person to apparently try it was Wan-Hu, a Chinese who was far ahead of his time. One day around the year 1500, Wan-Hu tied himself and forty-seven rockets to a chair and attempted to blast off. Unfortunately, he burned himself up and never left the ground.

Through the centuries, scientists in other countries talked and wrote about the possibilities of space travel. They drew diagrams and published their theories. Some built experimental rockets that used solid fuel. But solid-fuel rockets were incapable of space travel because of their dependence on oxygen. What was needed was a rocket that relied on a liquid fuel.

Robert H. Goddard stands beside his liquid-fuel rocket before its launching at Auburn, Massachusetts, on March 16, 1926. The liquid-fuel rocket made space travel possible.

One early scientist did envision such a rocket. Konstantin E. Tsiolkovsky, a Russian high school teacher, wrote about the possibilities of space travel in 1903. He even thought humans might someday establish colonies on the planets. But even though he wrote about liquid-fueled rockets, he made no attempt to build one.

The Liquid-Fueled Rocket

The first liquid-fueled rocket is credited to American scientist Robert H. Goddard. On March 16, 1926, he launched a 10-foot (3-meter) rocket from a farm in Auburn, Massachusetts. The rocket rose to a height of 41 feet (12.5 meters) before it crashed. From this humble beginning, the American space program was born.

Like many scientists, Goddard was ahead of his time. It was difficult for people in the 1920s to believe space travel was possible. Goddard was ridiculed and called by some "the moon rocket man." Residents on nearby farms where he carried out his tests complained about missiles whizzing all around them. They feared for the safety of their families.

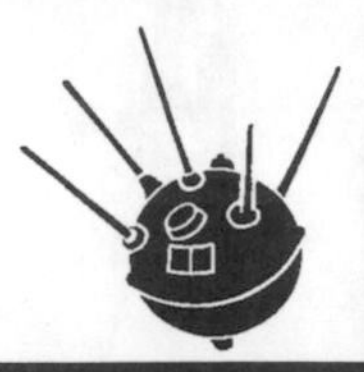

Goddard found a more isolated area and continued testing. He later moved his experiments to Roswell, New Mexico. As each year passed, he developed larger and more powerful rockets. In 1935 he launched the first rocket to go faster than the speed of sound. By the start of World War II, Goddard could send a rocket a mile into the air.

During World War II, the Germans made great advancements in rocketry. They developed the V-2 guided missile and used it against the Allies. After the war, many of the German scientists who worked on the V-2 were taken to the Soviet Union and forced to work for the Russians. Others came to the United States. These German scientists helped start the space programs in both countries.

Sputnik I, history's first man-made satellite, weighed 8,000 pounds (3,628 kilograms). It was launched by the Soviet Union on October 4, 1957.

The First Satellites

The race for space that began after World War II was won by the Russians. On October 4, 1957, the Soviet Union successfully launched *Sputnik I.* It was the first man-made satellite to be placed in orbit. About a month later, the Russians launched *Sputnik II.* It carried a small dog named Laika. Laika was the first living thing to travel in space.

Two months after the Soviet Union's achievements, the United States entered the Space Age. On January 31, 1958, America's first satellite, *Explorer I,* was put into orbit. Congress in the same year established the National Aeronautics and Space Administration (NASA) to oversee the American space program.

Human-Occupied Spacecraft

The Russians also launched the first human-occupied space vehicle. On April 12, 1961, Soviet cosmonaut (astronaut) Yuri Gagarin orbited Earth once in *Vostok I.* His flight lasted 1 hour and 48 minutes.

America was not far behind. On May 5 of the same year, Alan Shepard in *Mercury 4* was sent 300 miles (483 kilometers) downrange in a flight that lasted 15 minutes. Although *Mercury 4* was not placed in orbit, it represented the first time an American had ridden in a spacecraft.

America's first human-occupied orbital flight occurred on February 20, 1962. Marine Lt. Col. John H. Glenn circled Earth three times. His *Friendship 7* capsule stayed in orbit for 4 hours and 55 minutes. Glenn's flight

made him a national hero. He was honored by parades and public appearances. He was also invited to speak before a joint session of Congress.

Astronaut Edwin Aldrin walks on the moon on July 20, 1969. He and astronaut Neil Armstrong became the first humans to set foot on the moon's surface.

The First Moon Landing

America took the lead in the race for the moon. Between December 1968 and July 1969, three Apollo spacecraft came close to the moon's surface. *Apollo 10* actually got within 9 miles (14.5 kilometers). These three flights paved the way for *Apollo 11*'s historic feat in the summer of 1969.

Apollo 11 carried a crew of three. They were Neil Armstrong, Edward Aldrin, and Michael Collins. On July 20, Armstrong and Aldrin touched down on the moon in a strange-looking lunar vehicle called the *Eagle*. They spent about 2½ hours collecting rock samples and setting up instruments. Astronaut Collins remained in the command module while Armstrong and Aldrin were on the moon.

There were seven Apollo moon flights in all. Only *Apollo 13* in 1970 failed to reach its destination. An explosion of an oxygen tank caused the mission to be canceled. The three astronauts on board, however, were unharmed. They switched to the lunar module's oxygen supply and guidance system, and made it back to Earth. In 1995, a hit motion picture was made of the flight of *Apollo 13*.

The Space Shuttle

America scored another first in 1981. On April 12, the space shuttle *Columbia* lifted off from Cape Canaveral, Florida. On board were astronauts John Young and Robert Crippen. They circled the Earth 36 times, staying in orbit 54 hours. They returned safely and landed at Edwards Air Force Base in California on April 14.

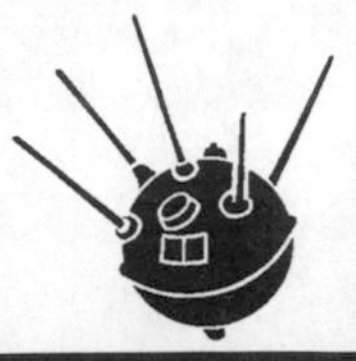

The space shuttle *Columbia* lifts off at Cape Canaveral on April 12, 1981, launching a new era in space exploration. The shuttle is the first reusable spacecraft to be put into orbit.

The shuttle program continued for five years with nothing but successes. Five space shuttles were built. Besides *Columbia,* there were *Challenger, Discovery, Atlantis,* and *Enterprise.* Between April 1981 and January 1986, seventeen shuttles were launched without incident. Then, on January 28, 1986, tragedy struck. The shuttle *Challenger* exploded 74 seconds after lift-off. All seven crew members were killed. One was Christa McAuliffe, a Massachusetts schoolteacher.

The *Challenger* disaster caused the shuttle program to be temporarily shut down. No flights were launched for over 2½ years. The program did not resume until all safety measures were checked and improved. It was not until September 1988, that another shuttle mission took off from Cape Canaveral.

By 1997, NASA had launched more than thirty shuttle flights. The astronauts and scientists involved have carried out a variety of missions. They have performed scientific and biological experiments. They have put satellites into orbit and retrieved others. They have repaired satellites like the Hubble space telescope, which was put into orbit in 1990 by the shuttle *Discovery.* And they have successfully docked in orbit with *Mir,* the Russian space station.

The space shuttle was the first reusable spacecraft to be built. It is launched like a rocket and glides to a landing like an airplane. It is designed to be flown as many as one hundred times. In the future, it will be used by NASA to construct a permanent station in space. It will carry supplies to this station and shuttle its occupants to and from Earth.

To be sure, the space shuttle makes the future of space exploration exciting. It might be used someday to build a craft capable of taking people and materials far into the deepest regions of the galaxy.

Name ______________________________ *Date* ____________________

Conduct an Interview

America has had its ups and downs in the space program. No one will ever forget the sorrow the nation felt when three astronauts died in a fire at Cape Canaveral in 1967. Or when the *Challenger* space shuttle blew up in January 1986.

But America's successes have far outweighed the failures. Americans beamed with pride over John Glenn's flight in 1961 and *Apollo 11*'s trip to the moon in 1969.

Interview an adult about his or her thoughts and feelings when the two events listed at right occurred. Write your findings on the lines provided.

Astronauts Armstrong and Aldrin's walk on the moon

The explosion of the Challenger

Name ______________________ *Date* ______________

Use Your Critical Thinking Skills

Think about the three questions presented below. Then write your best answer to each. Use a separate sheet of paper if necessary.

1. Until the fifteenth century, goods coming to Europe from Asia traveled long routes that were mostly over land. Such routes were dangerous and caused the price of Eastern goods to be very high. To acquire these luxuries at a reasonable price, Europeans began to look for an all-water route to the East. Their search eventually led to their discovery of the Americas, what they termed the "New World," in 1492.

   Can you think of any ways the present age of space exploration is similar to the Age of Exploration and Discovery that took place in the fifteenth and sixteenth centuries?

   ____

   ____

   ____

   Can you point out ways in which the two are different?

   ____

   ____

   ____

2. Do you think beings who resemble us in form exist on other planets? Why or why not?

   ____

   ____

   ____

3. Some people believe the government spends too much money on the space program. They think this money can better be used to solve important problems such as crime and poverty.

   What do you think? Do you agree or disagree? Give reasons why you feel the way you do.

   ____

   ____

   ____

Name ______________________ Date ______________

Solve a Puzzle About Space

Complete the sentences at the bottom of the page and then fill in missing letters to complete the spacecraft puzzle.

1. __________ are the initials of the National Aeronautics and Space Administration.
2. __________ I was the first satellite to be placed in orbit.
3. Yuri __________ was the first human to travel in space.
4. Robert Goddard invented the liquid-fuel __________ .
5. John __________ was the first American in space.
6. *Columbia* is one of the __________ shuttles.
7. Satellites are placed in __________ around the Earth.
8. __________ was the Russian dog who traveled in space.
9. __________ (how many) space shuttles had been built by 1997.
10. Yuri Gagarin's spacecraft was called __________ I.

___ ___ **S** ___

___ **P** ___ ___ ___ ___ ___

___ **A** ___ ___ ___ ___ ___

___ ___ **C** ___ ___ ___

___ ___ **E** ___ ___

___ ___ ___ **C** ___

___ **R** ___ ___ ___

___ **A** ___ ___ ___

F ___ ___ ___

___ ___ ___ **T** ___ ___

Name ______________________ Date ______________

Research the Solar System

Someday space adventurers may visit other planets in the solar system. The shuttle program has opened up possibilities that were not considered within reach a few decades ago. Who knows what the future holds in the world of space exploration.

Research the solar system in your science book or in an encyclopedia. Then answer the questions.

1. Write the names of the nine planets on the lines provided.

   ____

   ____

   ____

   ____

   ____

   ____

   ____

   ____

   ____

2. Which planet is nearest the sun? ______________
3. Which planet is farthest from the sun this year?

   ____
4. What giant galaxy is our solar system part of? ______________

In the space below, make a drawing of the solar system showing all of the planets in relation to the sun.

Answer Key

Chapter 1

Solve Some Math

1 a. 1,462,000 pounds (663,163 kilograms)
 b. about 1159%

2. 276 bales; 3,200 bales

Test Your Geography Skills

Maine/Augusta
New Hampshire/Concord
Vermont/Montpelier
Massachusetts/Boston
Rhode Island/Providence
Connecticut/Hartford

About Massachusetts

1. Vermont, New Hampshire
2. New York
3. Connecticut, Rhode Island
4. Boston

About Virginia

1. Tennessee, North Carolina
2. west

Chapter 2

Solve a Steamboat Puzzle

1. Hudson
2. Fitch
3. Five
4. Albany
5. Clermont
6. Submarine
7. Folly
8. Steam
9. Fulton

Test Your Math Skills

1. 4.69 mph (7.53 kph)
2. 1,996,000

Use Context Clues

Five Historic Airplanes

successful	feat	speed
attached	transatlantic	still
engine	hours	service
aloft	workhouse	traveled
distance	built	jointly
cause	passengers	

Chapter 3

Convert Scores to Morse Code

(Morse code):

•----	1	-••••	6
••---	2	--•••	7
•••--	3	---••	8
••••-	4	----•	9
•••••	5	-----	0

1.	Indians	••---
	Yankees	•----
2.	Red Sox	---••
	Blue Jays	•••--
3.	Dodgers	••••-
	Padres	-----
4.	Athletics	-••••
	Mariners	••---
5.	Rangers	•••••
	White Sox	••••-
6.	Braves	•----
	Reds	-----

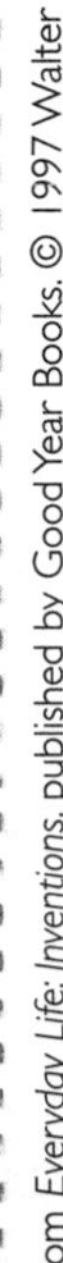

7.	Cubs	▬ ▬ • • •
	Marlins	• • ▬ ▬ ▬
8.	Mets	▬ ▬ ▬ ▬ •
	Phillies	• • • ▬ ▬
9.	Orioles	• • • • ▬
	Tigers	• ▬ ▬ ▬ ▬
10.	Astros	• • • ▬ ▬
	Cardinals	▬ ▬ ▬ ▬ ▬

Test Your Vocabulary

practical, Milwaukee; patent; handwritten; laborious; communicative; typewriters; expensive; produced, price; popular; manufacturers; combined, business; replaced

Use a Bar Graph to Compare Facts

1. 20 million
2. 4.5 million
3. Australia
4. 13

Chapter 4

Test Your Geography Knowledge

Hispaniola; Haiti, Dominican Republic; Port-au-Prince, Santo Domingo; Puerto Rico, United States; San Juan; Panama; Colombia, Costa Rica; Havana

Solve a Puzzle About Medicine

Across

1 Penicillin
3 Breathe
4 Polio
5 Antibiotic
6 Mosquitoes
10 Rutgers
11 Ether
12 Drinker

Down

2 Nobel
4 Pittsburgh
7 Surgery
8 Reed
9 Salk

Chapter 5

Use Context Clues to Complete Sentences

modern; dates; underwater; *Turtle;* powered; laughed; top; pilot; sink; planting; hull; failed; capsizing; escape; inventor; demonstrated; nation

Decide Which Word Does Not Belong

1. gun—A gun is not a shell.
2. rifle—A rifle is not a handgun.
3. Albert Einstein—Einstein was a scientist, not a U.S. President.
4. Ezra Lee—Ezra Lee was not an inventor.
5. submarine—A submarine can travel underwater.
6. Samuel Colt—Samuel Colt was not associated with the atomic bomb.
7. Hartford—Hartford is not a Japanese city.
8. Richard Gatling—Richard Gatling had nothing to do with submarines.
9. Nevada—Nevada is a state, not a country.

Solve Some Submarine Math

2. One knot equals about 1.15 mph (1.85 kph). Holland's submarine could travel 8.05 mph (12.9 kph) on the surface and 6.9 mph (11.1 kph) underwater.
3. Bonus. A nuclear-powered submarine does not rely on batteries underwater as do conventional submarines. This, together with it meeting less resistance underwater, enables it to travel faster.

Chapter 6

Solve These Math Problems

1 a. 6
  b. 360
  c. 2,880
2 a. 9.09 hours
  b. 7.27 hours
  c. 6.06 hours
3. $1,696.60

Test Your Critical Thinking Skills

1. Answers may vary.
2. Answers will vary, but should include such ideas as keeping records, producing report cards, providing activities for students in their individual classes, and so forth.
3. Bonus. Answers will vary, but most students will probably list calculators and microwave ovens.

Improve Your Map Skills

1. Hartford; north; New York; Albany; Rhode Island; Providence
2. southeastern; Albany; north; Adirondack; Massachusetts; Boston
3. Detroit; west or west northwest; Lansing; Indiana, Ohio, and Wisconsin
4. Europe; Spain; Belgium; Germany; Switzerland; Italy; Seine; English; Great Britain

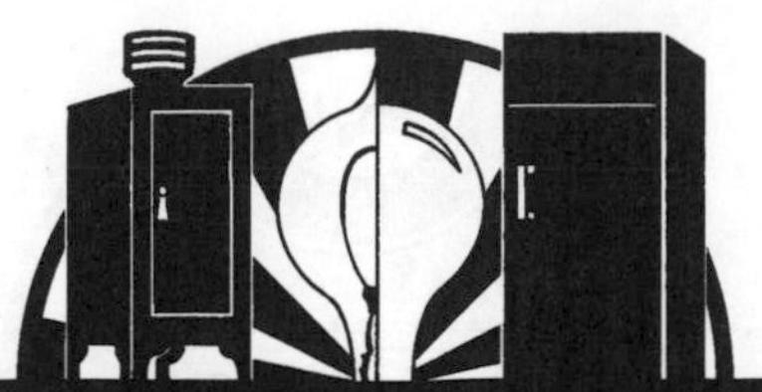

Complete a Word Search

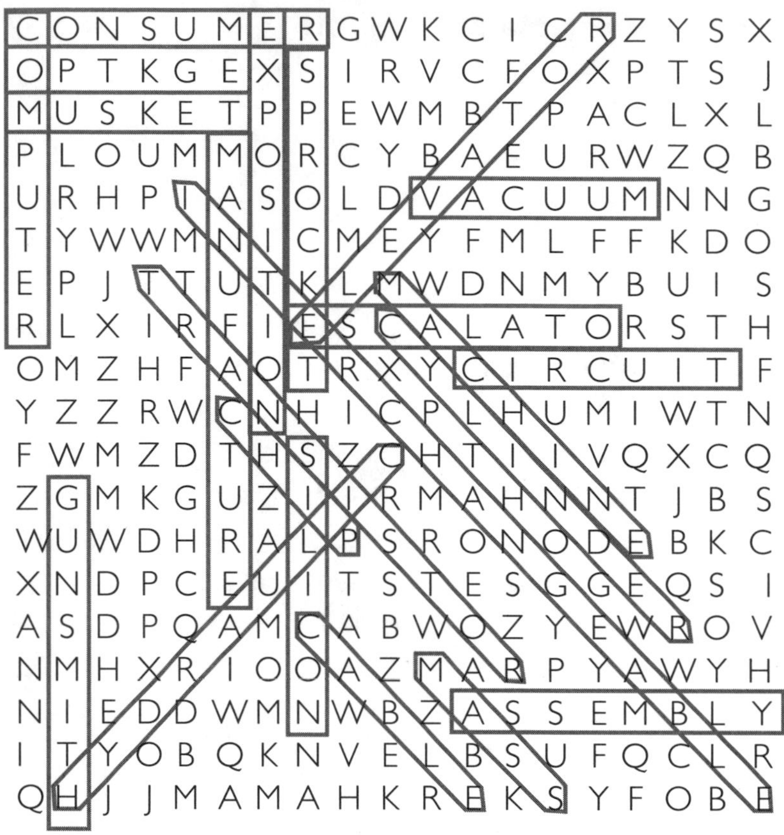

Chapter 7

Solve These Math Problems

1. 33 minutes
2. $40.20
3. 4 hours and 45 minutes
4. 41.67

Test Your Vocabulary

touched; progress, technology, enjoy, dreamed; cool; hot; vacuum; switch; clothes; comfortable; conveniences; next, bring; future, advanced

Chapter 8

Is TV Beneficial?

1. Answers will vary, but should include such things as entertaining, informative, relaxing, keeping up with current events, etc.
2. Answers will vary, but should include such criticisms as too much violence, inappropriate language and sexual scenes, television replacing family communication, etc.

Improve Your Geography Skills

1. St. Petersburg
2. Leningrad
3. St. Petersburg
4. Finland
5. Ladoga
6. Helsinki, Stockholm, Oslo
7. 4,140 miles (6,660 kilometers)

Broaden Your Vocabulary

1. see
2. far; over a long distance
3. of motion
4. instrument that writes, draws, or records
5. instrument for viewing or observing
6. picture or image
7. sound

Chapter 9

Solve a Consumer Products Crossword

Across
2 ivory
3 plastic
7 Birdseye
9 Hyatt
10 foil
11 Foods
13 fish

Down
1 vinyl
4 Swiss
5 Labrador
6 Reynolds
8 nylon
12 silk

Try These Word Problems

		Square Feet	Square Meters
1.	Size A	$.03	$.38
	Size B	$.02	$.26
	Size C	$.02	$.21

Size C is the best buy.

2. 200 feet (19 meters)
3. $1.26

Arrange in Chronological Order

1, 3, 8, 4, 7, 2, 6, 5

Test Your Vocabulary and Spelling Skills

cellophane; nylon; foil; plastic; vinyl; Formica

Chapter 10

Use Your Critical Thinking Skills

1. Similarities: Answers will vary, but should include ideas such as adventuresome, exciting, and explorations of unknown worlds.

   Differences: Answers will vary, but students should point out that space explorers have the advantage of advanced technology and a better knowledge of their destinations.
2. Answers may vary.
3. Answers may vary.

Solve a Puzzle About Space

1. NASA
2. Sputnik
3. Gagarin
4. rocket
5. Glenn
6. space
7. orbit
8. Laika
9. Five
10. Vostok

Research the Solar System

1. Mercury, Venus, Earth, Mars, Jupiter, Saturn, Uranus, Neptune, Pluto
2. Mercury
3. Neptune, until 1999, then Pluto.
4. Milky Way

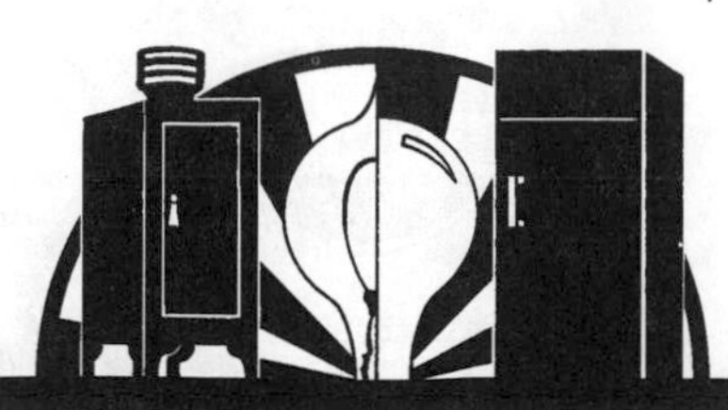

Additional Resources

Books for Children

Aaseng, Nathan. *The Inventors: Nobel Prizes in Chemistry, Physics, and Medicine.* Minneapolis, MN: Lerner Publications Company, 1988.

Bender, Lionel. *Inventions.* New York: Alfred A. Knopf, 1991.

Clarke, Donald, ed. *The Encyclopedia of Inventions.* New York: Galahad Books, 1977.

Holt, Michael. *Inventions.* Milwaukee, WI: Gareth Stevens Children's Books, 1990.

Markham, Lois. *Inventions That Changed Modern Life.* Austin, TX: Steck-Vaughn Publishers, 1994.

Parker, Steve. *The History of Medicine.* Milwaukee, WI: Gareth Stevens Children's Books, 1992.

Books for Adults

Peterson, Harold L. *The Treasury of the Gun.* New York: Golden Press, 1962.

Breeden, Robert L., ed. *Those Inventive Americans.* Washington, D.C.: National Geographic Society, 1971.